NATIONAL GEOGRAPHIC KIDS

WILDER PLANET

Published by Collins
An imprint of HarperCollins Publishers
Westerhill Road
Bishopbriggs
Glasgow G64 2QT
www.harpercollins.co.uk

HarperCollins Publishers
Macken House
39/40 Mayor Street
Upper Dublin 1
D01 C9W8
Ireland

In association with National Geographic Partners, LLC

NATIONAL GEOGRAPHIC and the Yellow Border Design are trademarks of the National Geographic Society, used under license.

First published 2024

Text copyright © 2024 HarperCollins Publishers.
All Rights Reserved.

ISBN 978-0-00-866450-3

10 9 8 7 6 5 4 3 2 1

All rights reserved. No part of this publication may be reproduced, stored in a retrieval system, or transmitted, in any form or by any means, electronic, mechanical, photocopying, recording or otherwise without the prior permission in writing of the publisher and copyright owners.

The contents of this publication are believed correct at the time of printing. Nevertheless the publisher can accept no responsibility for errors or omissions, changes in the detail given or for any expense or loss thereby caused.

A catalogue record for this book is available from the British Library.

Printed in India.

If you would like to comment on any aspect of this book, please contact us at the above address or online.
natgeokidsbooks.co.uk
collins.reference@harpercollins.co.uk

MIX
Paper | Supporting responsible forestry
FSC
www.fsc.org
FSC™ C007454

NATIONAL GEOGRAPHIC KiDS

WILDER PLANET

50 INCREDIBLE REWILDING PROJECTS

CONTENTS

UNITED KINGDOM... 6

EUROPE... 26

NORTH AMERICA... 52

SOUTH AMERICA... 66

4

AFRICA... 80

ASIA... 96

OCEANIA... 108

ANTARCTICA... 118

GLOSSARY... 122

UNITED KINGDOM

Find out about the **reintroduction of red squirrels** in **Wales** on page 22.

EALING BEAVER PROJECT

Natural England have given permission for a **pair of beavers** to be **introduced** to a carefully selected habitat at Paradise Fields in **London**.

This special rewilding project is being run by Ealing Wildlife Group and Ealing Council. In recent years, beavers have been introduced in other places around the UK, bringing back this iconic animal after it was hunted to near extinction 400 years ago. Beavers are now living wild in two areas in Scotland and one in Devon. Elsewhere, beavers have been introduced into enclosed areas so that the effects of their rewilding activities can be monitored.

The Ealing project will be an important study into what impact beavers may have on an urban landscape, so that we can understand what might happen and plan for when beavers move into more towns and cities.

Beavers are important animals because they transform areas into thriving wetlands, full of homes for many other species, including plants, insects, amphibians and water voles. This increases the biodiversity of the area and improves water quality.

BEAVER

ENGLAND, UK

DID YOU KNOW?

Beavers are known as 'ecosystem engineers' as their carefully constructed homes built on streams slow the flow of water. This stops flooding during heavy downpours, which can protect people's homes.

SUCCESS STORIES...

Ealing Wildlife Group have already helped bring back another native species to areas around London. **Harvest mice,** which had been extinct in the area for generations, have been found to be successfully breeding after their reintroduction.

HARVEST MOUSE

EUROPEAN BISON and the WILDER BLEAN PROJECT

European bison have been introduced to West Blean and Thornden Woods in Canterbury by Kent Wildlife Trust, as part of an effort to help restore and rewild the woodland habitat.

West Blean woods is one of the largest areas of ancient woodland in the UK and an ideal home for European bison.

Before Kent Wildlife Trust began managing the area, it was used for commercial timber production and had too many non-native conifer trees.

Bison, like beavers, are 'ecosystem engineers' whose natural behaviour helps the surrounding habitat. When these huge animals forage and move around the woodland they disturb the land, encouraging new growth of different species of plant and creating homes and food for smaller animals.

Exmoor ponies and Iron Age pigs (a hybrid of a wild boar and domestic pig) have also been introduced into the area. The hope is that these animals will provide even more benefit to the woodland for all to enjoy.

EXMOOR PONY

SUCCESS STORIES...

ENGLAND, UK

European bison were driven almost to extinction through hunting less than a century ago. They were saved only by captive breeding and rewilding projects in different areas across Europe.

These herbivores haven't roamed the woodlands of the UK for about 6,000 years, so bringing back even a small herd is a huge achievement for conservationists.

EUROPEAN BISON

DID YOU KNOW?
The European bison is the continent's largest land mammal.

KNEPP CASTLE ESTATE

Knepp Castle Estate in West Sussex was once home to a dairy farm, but since 2001, the landowners have stopped farming and successfully **rewilded 1,400 hectares.**

After a century of commercial farming, most of the sheep and cattle were removed from the site. This instantly reduced grazing pressure and allowed nature to reclaim the area.

The rewilding of Knepp is unusual. There is no specific goal and little human interaction since the fences that once divided the land were taken down. It is an experiment to see what happens when native breeds of cattle, pig, and pony and wild deer are allowed to move around freely to manage the landscape naturally.

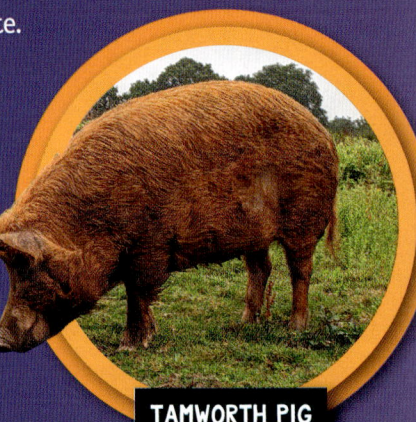

TAMWORTH PIG

After 20 years of allowing nature to 'go wild', Knepp has seen a huge increase in wildlife and is now a breeding hotspot for Critically Endangered nightingales and turtle doves.

NIGHTINGALE

SUCCESS STORIES...

ENGLAND, UK

Thirteen out of the UK's 17 breeding species of **bat** can all be found at Knepp, including two of the rarest species in Europe.

BARBASTELLE BAT

Knepp has the largest population of **purple emperor butterflies** in the United Kingdom.

PURPLE EMPEROR BUTTERFLY

In 2021, Knepp recorded seven nesting pairs of **White Storks,** with 14 chicks successfully fledged. Since then, more birds have gone on to breed and raise young, putting the rewilding team on track to reach a target of 50 breeding pairs by 2030.

WHITE STORKS

THE GREAT FEN

The Great Fen is an **ambitious, long-term** rewilding project in Cambridgeshire, **connecting** two nature reserves – Woodwalton Fen and Holme Fen – with the goal of managing the land for **nature** and for people to enjoy.

For over 20 years, the Wildlife Trust for Bedfordshire, Cambridgeshire and Northamptonshire and partners have been rewilding around 3,700 hectares of countryside. The group have connected the two nature reserves via wetland and created a haven for wildlife.

In 2023, the Peatland Progress project began. The projects involves restoring wetland in the area between the two reserves. This area was drained in the 1850s for peat production and farming, destroying 99% of the peatland.

Restoring this connecting land allows species to move between two large suitable habitats. The area is a demonstration site for a new land management system called 'wet farming'.

Crops such as the common bulrush (used as insulation and filling in clothes) and sphagnum moss (used by gardeners) can be farmed. This protects peat soils, while still providing a livelihood for local people.

Reducing peat loss here will save an estimated 325,000 tonnes of carbon dioxide from being released into the atmosphere and help fight the effects of climate change.

DID YOU KNOW?

The Great Fen is not only an important site for the environment, but is rich in history too. The Romans built a causeway across The Fens, and a coin dating to this period (138–181 CE) was found in the area in 1940.

BARN OWL

ENGLAND, UK

SUCCESS STORIES...

Common cranes disappeared from The Fen landscape around 400 years ago due to the pressures of hunting and habitat change, but since 2008 they have been spotted in Woodwalton Fen.

Avocets, snipes, lapwings, peregrine falcons and barn owls have all been sighted too and are successfully breeding in the area.

CRANE

AVOCET

REWILDING AFFRIC HIGHLANDS

A **massive** rewilding project is taking place in the heart of the **Scottish Highlands** where woodland, peatland, wetland and rivers are being **restored** to encourage native species, such as the **golden eagle** and **black grouse**, back into the area.

BLACK GROUSE

This 30-year rewilding project in Scotland sees Rewilding Europe and Trees for Life teaming up with local communities. The aim is to transform bare hillsides back into ancient Caledonian pinewood, and reconnect wooded areas so that wildlife can move more freely between them.

The landscape has suffered from overgrazing by animals such as sheep and deer, but by removing them and allowing natural regrowth, other animals have been allowed to return to a more natural ecosystem.

SCOTTISH HIGHLANDS

With more trees growing, rivers are more shaded. This benefits fish to spawn and their fry to thrive. Rewetting of peatlands not only helps tackle the climate crisis (they act as carbon sinks) but also provides habitat for invertebrates and birds.

Rewilding this part of Scotland not only helps animals and the environment but has been inspiring people to reconnect with nature and has helped boost the local economy.

SUCCESS STORIES...

Trees for Life have planted around **2 million native trees** at different sites around the Highlands, helping to restore the Caledonian forest.

Thanks to the success of rewilding, Affric Highlands contains some of the best places to spot **golden eagles, red squirrels, otters** and **pine martens.**

SCOTLAND, UK

GOLDEN EAGLE

DID YOU KNOW?

Peatlands make up a tiny fraction of habitat around the world, but they store more than double the amount of carbon of all the world's forests put together! So they are very important habitats to protect.

OTTER

SAVING WILDCATS

DID YOU KNOW?
Scottish wildcats are known as 'Highland tigers'.

The **Scottish wildcat** is one on the UK's most **threatened** mammals. Saving Wildcats' **aim** is to **restore** Scotland's wildcat population across the country and **prevent extinction**.

The wildcat was once widespread across the UK. However, habitat loss and hunting wiped this species out in England and Wales in the late 1800s, and it only remained in Scotland.

The biggest threat to the Scottish wildcat now is breeding with domestic cats. This creates hybrid kittens. This is such a problem that it is thought there are now no longer any 'true' wildcats left in Scotland.

Wildcats have an important role in the landscape: they prey on small animals, keeping numbers in check and helping to maintain balance in the ecosystem. They will be important inhabitants of Scotland's rewilded landscapes.

The Saving Wildcats' recovery project is breeding Scottish wildcats for release in the Cairngorms National Park, returning this important predator back to its habitat.

SUCCESS STORIES...

In 2022, **22 kittens** were born at the centre. With wildcats being one of the most endangered animals in the UK, each kitten is a lifeline for the future of the species.

These young cats will be taught how to **survive** in the wild and, over time, will be released and monitored, contributing directly to rewilding in Scotland.

SCOTLAND, UK

WILDCAT KITTEN

PINE MARTEN RECOVERY PROJECT

For more than **30 years** Vincent Wildlife Trust (VWT) has helped **pine martens recover** in areas across the UK by bringing individuals from **Scotland** to suitable habitats south of the border.

Pine martens once roamed wild in woodland throughout the UK. However, habitat loss and being hunted during Victorian times massively reduced their numbers. While populations gradually managed to recover naturally in Scotland, without help, pine martens in England and Wales were so few they were threatened with extinction.

Pine martens are predators that hunt in the trees. They may have an extra special role to play in rewilding the UK's woodlands. They feed mostly on the prey they can find most easily in the trees, which is likely to include grey squirrels. Grey squirrels spread disease to native red squirrels and outcompete them for food and habitat. By reducing grey squirrel numbers, pine martens can give native red squirrels a helping paw.

VWT has boosted three small Welsh populations with pine martens from Scotland, and helped monitor areas in northern England because pine martens have spread south from Scotland and crossed the border on their own.

Pine martens are making a comeback in other parts of England too. A population was discovered in Shropshire in 2015. And between 2019 and 2021, 35 were translocated to the Forest of Dean by VWT and partners.

DID YOU KNOW?

Despite their name, pine martens are at home in broadleaved woodlands as well as natural pine forests.

ENGLAND AND WALES, UK

SUCCESS STORIES...

The **translocated pine martens** (those moved from Scotland to Wales) have continued to establish themselves, and breeding has been recorded every year since the first animals were moved by the Trust in 2015.

In 2023, pine marten kits were **caught on film** in the Forest of Dean, evidence that the new population is breeding successfully.

PINE MARTEN

REINTRODUCTION of RED SQUIRRELS

Wildwood Trust is one of a number of **conservation groups** working to bring the **red squirrel** back to areas around **Wales**.

Red squirrels were once a common sight all over the UK. However, in the 1800s, they were almost wiped out when Victorians introduced non-native grey squirrels to Britain.

Red squirrel populations are falling as the grey squirrels outcompete them for food. Grey squirrels also carry the squirrel pox virus, which is deadly to native red squirrels.

Red squirrels can now only be found in certain areas of Scotland, Ireland and in limited areas in England and Wales. However, even in these areas they are at risk due to habitat loss and the growing presence of grey squirrels.

Since 2002, Wildwood Trust has been breeding red squirrels to be released in selected sites in Wales, bringing back this iconic species to the country. Areas include the island of Anglesey, Gwynedd and Clocaenog Forest.

SUCCESS STORIES...

For over 20 years, Wildwood Trust have bred around **six squirrels** a year. These squirrels have been released and monitored, boosting local populations.

RED SQUIRREL

WALES, UK

DID YOU KNOW?

Red squirrels are not always red in colour – their coats can be black, brown or even white!

UK STURGEON PROJECT

The UK Sturgeon Alliance, formed in 2020, is made up of organisations such as the Zoological Society of London (ZSL) and Blue Marine Foundation that are **determined** to **restore native sturgeon** species to UK waters.

Two species of sturgeon were once common in UK waters – the Atlantic sturgeon and the now Critically Endangered European sturgeon. Their numbers have fallen drastically over many years. This is due to habitat destruction and pollution, as well as the building of dams which stop fish moving to spawning grounds.

The last officially recorded river capture of a sturgeon by fishers was in 1993 in the River Tywi in Wales. These fish are now so rare in UK waters, the UK Sturgeon Alliance are asking the public to record sturgeon sightings to gather data on these species.

EUROPEAN STURGEON

UNITED KINGDOM

To help restore sturgeon populations, organisations are working together to reduce pollution in rivers and estuaries where young sturgeons gather. These groups are also restoring gravel beds in freshwater where the adults spawn. Additionally, the removal of weirs (small barriers built across rivers to control the water level) that are no longer in use, is helping fish migrate.

DID YOU KNOW?

The sturgeon is the largest fish that can live in both freshwater and marine environments in the UK. The European sturgeon can grow to 8 metres in length and both UK species can live for up to 100 years.

SUCCESS STORIES...

Thanks to long-term **reintroduction projects** in France and Germany, alongside the UK Sturgeon Alliance's efforts, sturgeon have been returning to UK coasts in recent years, giving hope for the future of this iconic fish.

EUROPE

Find out about **pelicans** returning to the **River Danube Delta** in **Ukraine** on page 50.

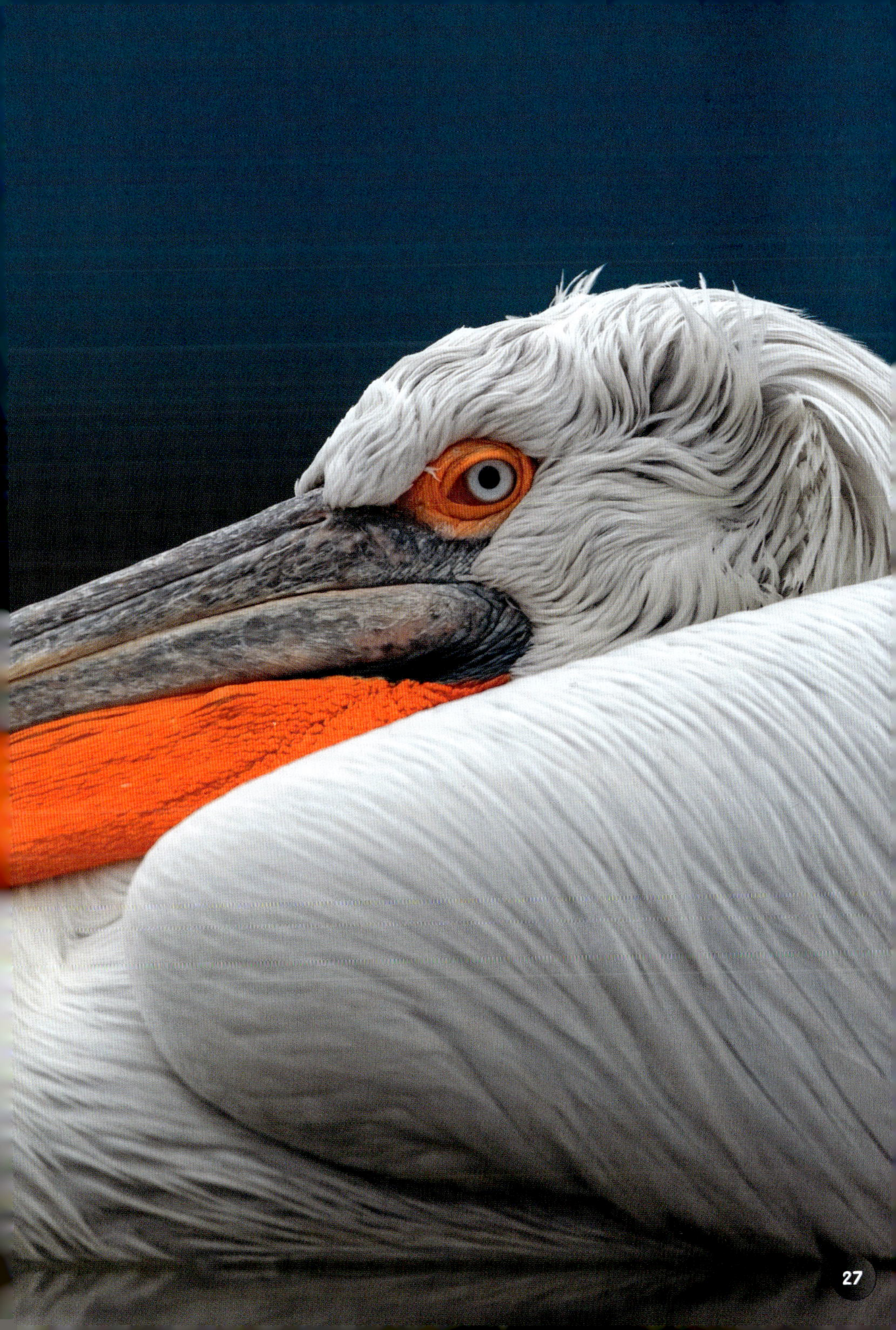

RHODOPE MOUNTAINS REWILDING

The **Rhodope Mountains** in **Bulgaria** contain a range of **habitats** and are home to a huge number of **plant** and **animal** species.

The Rewilding Rhodope team are focused on managing the land naturally. They are increasing the biodiversity in the landscape by restoring populations of the types of large herbivores that used to roam the area.

Grazing trials are taking place with free-roaming wild horses and European bison. This will allow scientists to study how large numbers of grazing animals affect the habitat, and determine whether their introduction to certain areas will improve the landscape.

RHODOPE MOUNTAINS

GOLDEN JACKAL

BULGARIA

Another focus of the project is to help threatened species of vulture. Increasing grazing animals, including red and fallow deer, increases the number of carcasses available as the herbivores die. This provides these declining birds, and other scavengers, such as the golden jackal, with a natural food source, helping to increase their numbers.

Rewilding Rhodope is also enhancing the landscape as a nature-tourism destination. This supports local communities and promotes the Rhodope Mountains in a sustainable way.

RED DEER

SUCCESS STORIES...

There are nearly **200 Karakachan** and **Konik horses** moving around the landscape. These herbivores are maintaining natural meadows, helping new growth of plants and trees, and providing a food source for other animals.

KONIK HORSES

Deer populations are increasing in a sustainable way through species management and more than **15 European bison,** introduced in 2019, are thriving in the area, with the birth of four calves in 2022.

EUROPEAN BISON

BRINGING BACK THE DUNG BEETLE

An initiative supported by the European Wildlife Comeback Fund saw the **release** of around **60 dung beetles** in southwest France. The aim was to **improve** soil quality in the area and help to **increase biodiversity** across the landscape.

DUNG BEETLE ▸▸▸

DID YOU KNOW?
Dung beetles can be found on every continent except Antarctica.

FRANCE

The dung beetle *Scarabaeus laticollis* was released into an area of southwest France called the Landes De Gascogne (Gascony Moors), an area of coastal wetland and forest, as part of a rewilding project.

The site is grazed by Marine-Landaise cattle, a breed that is specially adapted to the area and whose grazing manages the moors in a natural way. The dung beetles are a critical part of rewilding the area because they process the cattle's dung within the natural ecosystem. They do this by rolling the dung into balls and pushing the balls to underground chambers for their larvae to feast on. This improves the biodiversity of the soil above and below ground.

As they grow in number, the beetles will be an additional food source for birds and small mammals. Initially, though, the released beetles were protected from predators until they had established underground burrows.

With the loss of wild grazing animals in open habitat, and habitat change to make way for farming, the dung beetle population has declined across Europe. With rewilding projects bringing back large herbivores to naturally manage wild spaces, returning their companion species is the natural next step.

SUCCESS STORIES...

This species hadn't been seen in the area since 1965, due to the decline of large herbivores who provide them with a food source. The reintroduction of this insect is a great conservation success.

URBAN REWILDING in GERMANY

In 2020, a project launched by The Nature Conservancy's Urban Greening Programme in **Berlin** used **sheep** to manage land and **increase biodiversity**.

Wilmersdorf Stadium in the heart of Berlin was built in the mid-twentieth century as an athletics facility. Due to lack of use, the facility's old seats were removed in the 1990s and, over time, the embankment was claimed by hard-to-control weeds.

Conservationists suggested the use of sheep to control weed growth through grazing the embankments. The hope was to enhance urban biodiversity while also testing a cheap and eco-friendly form of landscape maintenance.

By grazing the overgrown area, the sheep would allow a more diverse grassy habitat to develop. This would support an increased variety of insects, birds and other wildlife into the busy city of Berlin.

Urban rewilding is important, as some at-risk species show higher rates of reproduction success (raising young to adulthood) in urban areas than in rural ones — such as the peregrine falcon.

Reclaimed green pockets in cities have the potential to boost species' populations and tackle the effects of climate change if they are managed properly. Projects such as those carried out in Berlin are showing the way for future urban rewilding.

SHEEP

SUCCESS STORIES...

BERLIN

GERMANY

DID YOU KNOW?

It is thought there are more fox dens within the city of Berlin than in surrounding forest.

In Berlin, **bicycles** make up **13%** of all traffic, helping to lower emissions and reduce pollution in the city.

FOX

Urban beehives are being installed on the roofs of buildings to increase the number of pollinators.

URBAN BEEKEEPING IN BERLIN

33

THE AUERRIND PROJECT

The **Auerrind Project** started in 2013 and is a rewilding effort focusing on **natural grazing** using a modern-day equivalent animal to a now **extinct ancestor** of modern cattle, known as the **aurochs**.

The aurochs was a huge herbivore standing 6 foot tall and weighing the same as a family car. The species roamed across Eurasia and North Africa for 250,000 years but were hunted to extinction by humans. The last known aurochs died in Poland in 1627.

The aurochs may have been lost hundreds of years ago, but traces of their DNA can be found in a number of ancient cattle breeds found in different parts of the world. Scientists have analysed the DNA so that they can 'back-breed' from an animal as close to the aurochs as possible, by breeding only animals that share traits with them, such as how they look and how they behave.

Based at the Lauresham Laboratory for Experimental Archaeology in Germany, the Auerrind Project also wants to raise awareness of the necessity for large herbivores to naturally manage landscapes.

Their vision is to increase knowledge of the extinct aurochs and successfully back-breed to a grazing animal that will fulfil the role of the aurochs, creating a varied ever-changing landscape that supports a natural range of plants and animals.

DID YOU KNOW?

Scientists are also working on bringing back other extinct animals including the passenger pigeon, Tasmanian tiger and woolly mammoth!

STRANDS OF AUROCHS' DNA CAN STILL BE FOUND IN SOME ANCIENT EUROPEAN CATTLE, SUCH AS TAUROS CATTLE.

GERMANY

SUCCESS STORIES...

Scientists have established **five breeding herds** in meadows in Austria and Germany with new expansions of land and breeding bulls planned in 2023–2024.

The **third generation** of these animals show remarkable similarities to their ancient predecessors. The largest bull in the Auerrind herd stands just shy of 6 feet and has horns that would rival those of aurochs bulls.

RETURN of the MOST ENDANGERED SEAL on EARTH

The **Mediterranean monk seal** is one of the **rarest** marine mammals on Earth, with only around **600 left** in the wild.

The Eastern Adriatic Monk Seal Project began in 2017. It was started to tackle the challenges facing the Critically Endangered monk seal along the coastline of Greece.

Pollution, habitat destruction and deliberate killing by fishers throughout the last century has led to their disappearance. In addition, monk seals face threats due to human disturbance of marine caves, which they use to rest in and give birth to their young. Tourist development has forced the seals to raise their pups in different caves that are unsuitable, leading to a low pup survival rate.

The Eastern Adriatic Monk Seal Project hopes to reverse these effects by identifying and protecting caves used by seals. They are raising awareness of the seals' struggles, in cooperation with locals, the fishing industry and tourist operators, so that the project is successful in the long term.

Greece has more than 16,000 kilometres of coastline and has the potential to be a good home for monk seals. A small population live there already, and is growing in number thanks to conservation groups. The project hopes to increase this number by protecting more of the seals' habitat.

If enough coastline can be restored and protected, it is hoped the seals will eventually spread back into their former range along the coasts north of Greece — in Albania, Montenegro and Croatia.

GREECE

SUCCESS STORIES...

The project is now in Phase 2, after Phase 1 successfully showed that conditions along the Greek coast are suitable for populations to expand. Phase 2 will focus on monitoring the seals' movement along the coast and finding more areas of suitable habitat, whilst continuing to raise awareness.

DID YOU KNOW?

Most seals live in areas close to the North and South Pole. Only a few, such as the California sea lion, Hawaiian monk seal and Mediterranean monk seal, have adapted to live in warmer environments.

MEDITERRANEAN MONK SEAL

WILD NEPHIN NATIONAL PARK

Wild Nephin National Park in County Mayo, Ireland, is undergoing a rewilding programme to allow its **bog** and **forest** to return to their **natural state**. With its hands-off conservation approach, this is the **first project of its kind** in the country.

In the middle of Wild Nephin National Park, the Owenduff bog stretches for miles. This large area of wetland is one of the last intact blanket bogs left in western Europe. As a type of peatland, it is a key store of carbon. The plan to rewild it back to its natural state includes the removal of conifers and blocking up forest drains to retain water in the area.

OWENDUFF BOG

The national park was established in 1998 and renamed Wild Nephin after the Nephin Beg Mountain Range. In 2017, it was extended when around 4,000 hectares of commercial plantation was taken over to rewild.

Thousands of native trees have since been planted throughout the landscape, including sessile oak, birch, rowan, Scots pine and many more. Removing invasive rhododendron (a type of shrub) and closing forest roads will also help increase the biodiversity of the landscape.

After these initial steps are taken, the landscape will be left alone by conservationists and allowed to develop and thrive naturally — a first conservation effort of its kind in the country.

WILD NEPHIN NATIONAL PARK

IRELAND

SUCCESS STORIES...

Birds like the **golden plover** and **red grouse** have been seen returning to the park in higher numbers and nesting since the programme began.

RED GROUSE

DID YOU KNOW?

Wild Nephin National Park is home to Ireland's first International Dark Sky Park. It has some of the clearest, twinkling skies in the world and attracts star-gazers from all over.

GOLDEN PLOVER

LIFE BEAR SMART CORRIDORS

In **Europe**, four of the ten populations of **brown bear** are classed as **Critically Endangered**.

MARSICAN BEAR, ITALY

LIFE Bear-Smart Corridors is a project to help grow populations of Europe's brown bears in central Italy and Greece through the development of 'wildlife corridors'.

In the Rhodope and Pindos mountain ranges in Greece, the combined bear population is down to between 400 and 500 individuals. The Apennines in Italy are home to an endemic subspecies known as the Marsican brown bear, which is at even greater risk.

The initiative hopes to extend the environments the bears occupy by rewilding areas of land connecting the national parks where they currently live. These wildlife corridors will make the area each bear can roam bigger.

Rewilding the landscape to support natural food sources, like fungi and berries, reduces the likelihood of bears being attracted into towns and villages in search of food scraps. The corridors will be part of efforts to encourage local communities to live alongside these large animals and reduce conflict between them.

DID YOU KNOW?
There are only around 60 Marsican brown bears left in the wild.

SUCCESS STORIES...

ITALY and GREECE

LIFE Bear-Smart Corridors' first test was the creation of a **wildlife corridor** in the Apennines. In just three years, this corridor has seen a 99% reduction in bear damage to local people's property and an increase in cubs born within the local bear population.

The project is an adaptation of the Bear Smart Community project that has been successfully carried out in Canada.

MARSICAN BEAR CUBS, ITALY

THE GELDERSE POORT PROJECT

The Gelderse Poort Project was a unique effort to use **nature conservation** to help **solve modern-day problems**. The River Waal, in the Nijmegen area in the Netherlands, was **restored** and floodplain created for the river to expand into, helping to **reduce damage** caused by flooding.

The project reclaimed and rewilded areas of floodplain for the River Waal to flood into during periods of high rainfall. This reduced the risk of homes being flooded, as well as providing more wetland habitat for wildlife.

Previously, the local community was protected against burst riverbanks and rising water levels by dykes (a wall or embankment built to protect against flooding). These didn't always work and major floods in 1993 and 1995, forced over a quarter of a million people out of their homes. Rather than just building more barriers against the floods, the new project created space for the water to disperse naturally without causing damage. This solution to the major issue of flooding was eco-friendly and sustainable in the long term.

CATTLE GRAZING THE FLOODPLAIN

NETHERLANDS

A century ago, these areas were floodplains, full of natural marshes. However, farmers drained them over time to grow crops. The new channels and floodplain are an example of rewilding by recreating the landscape that existed before.

This project is an exampe of how rewilding can benefit not just wildlife but people too. The Gelderse Poort Project is now a source of inspiration for the restoration of other rivers in Europe.

DID YOU KNOW?

Climate change has made extreme weather events, such as floods, more common and more severe.

SUCCESS STORIES...

Nijmegen was awarded the title of **European Green Capital** in 2018, the first Dutch city to achieve this. The title is awarded every year to a European city that leads the way in sustainability.

FLOODPLAINS, RIVER WAAL

BRINGING BACK the IBERIAN LYNX

The **Iberian lynx** almost became **extinct** but thanks to recent conservation efforts the **population** has **increased** across **southwest Europe**.

Fifty years ago, the Iberian Peninsula (the part of Europe containing Portugal and Spain) was home to thousands of Iberian lynx. But, by 2002, the creature was extinct in Portugal, and fewer than 100 were left in Spain. Causes for this decline included:

- being hunted for their pelts
- habitat loss
- collisions with vehicles
- declining rabbit numbers, which make up around 75% of the lynx's diet
- being killed by farmers protecting their livestock.

Without help from conservation groups, this animal would have been lost forever.

Reintroducing the lynx to the wild could only be successful if the threats to them were reduced. Organisations got to work rewilding farmland to boost prey numbers and create 'wildlife corridors' to join up areas of suitable habitat, as well as building highway tunnels underneath busy roads so that the lynx could avoid crossing them. Four captive breeding centres were set up, three in Spain and one in Portugal, to breed them for release into the wild.

The conservation efforts paid off, and in 2016 the first captive-bred lynx were released in Portugal. Now over 1,000 Iberian lynx live on the peninsula.

DID YOU KNOW?

The Iberian lynx is the world's most endangered feline species.

SUCCESS STORIES...

PORTUGAL and SPAIN

Seventy lynx kittens were born in 2021 in Guadiana Valley National Park in Portugal, which now has a stable population in the country.

Rewilding Europe have set aside more than **100 square kilometres** of land in the Greater Côa Valley, also in Portugal, for rewilding, including bringing back the Iberian lynx, and supporting endangered populations of ibex and Iberian wolves.

IBEX

IBERIAN LYNX

SAVING the ANGELS of the ATLANTIC

Angelshark Project: Canary Islands formed in 2013 to help **protect** the **Critically Endangered angelshark** in its last stronghold in the waters around the **Spanish Canary Islands**.

Three angelshark species were once found in Europe's seas — the angelshark, sawback angelshark and smoothback angelshark. However, this family of sharks is now extinct from much of their former range. New fishing techniques and overfishing in many areas have reduced their food sources, and their coastal habitats have been damaged by pollution and human activity. As these animals are very slow to reproduce, the loss of just one individual can impact the whole population.

Limited understanding of adult angelshark behaviour has been a major obstacle to protecting them, but this is improving every year. Visual and electronic tagging is being used by the Angelshark Project team to monitor their movements and increase understanding of angelsharks and their behaviour. Fishers and members of the public have been recording sightings of angelsharks too. Collecting data about the angelsharks' population and environment, enables them to offer better conservation in the Canary Islands.

Like all shark species, the angelshark keeps balance in the ecosystem. They do this by removing weak and diseased fish, helping to maintain the health of prey species, so losing the angelshark would have negative consequences for biodiversity around the Canary Islands.

SPAIN

SUCCESS STORIES...

In 2019, **angelsharks** were added to the **Spanish Endangered Species List** for the Canary Island waters. This means that any action that may cause harm to this species of fish, such as catching them while fishing for other species or disturbing their habitat, is strictly prohibited.

ANGELSHARK

DID YOU KNOW?

In 2014, the angelshark family was identified as one of the three most threatened of all the world's sharks and rays.

REWILDING LAPLAND

Rewilding Lapland hopes to **restore forest** and **rivers** in **Lapland** to help both **wildlife** and indigenous communities such as the **Sámi people.**

REINDEER

SWEDEN

Reindeer migration and free-flowing river systems shape the landscape of Swedish Sápmi (the Sámi name for Lapland) and are also a key part of people's way of life there. The Sámi have herded reindeer for hundreds of years. It is a major occupation in the area and is considered an important tradition to keep alive.

The movement and grazing behaviour of the reindeer helps new growth of grasses, plants and trees. This increases the biodiversity of Lapland's forests.

Modern day obstacles are restricting the migration of the reindeer. The building of mines, roads and dams make it harder for the reindeer to move around the land. Forests have been cleared, leaving behind less of the food that the reindeer need, such as lichen. This negatively impacts people and wildlife.

Rewilding Lapland is dedicated to restoring the old-growth forests and removing obstructions in rivers. This helps wildlife move freely between areas to search for food and to reproduce. The organisation is also helping to find other opportunities for sustainable development that can co-exist with nature and local communities.

DID YOU KNOW?

There are more reindeer than people in Sápmi!

SUCCESS STORIES...

Rewilding Lapland has received grants from the Swedish Government in recent years. They have used this money to **rewild forests** and to restore **60 spawning grounds** (where fish lay eggs) along a 12-kilometre stretch of the River Abramsån.

RESTORING the DANUBE DELTA

Rewilding Europe is **driving restoration** efforts in Europe's **largest wetland** area – where the Danube River meets the Black Sea. This massive delta is home to large numbers of **waterbirds**.

The Danube Delta provides an essential habitat for birds such as pelicans, herons, storks and terns. The delta is an important wintering ground (the place where migratory animals live when they are not breeding) for lots of other migrating waterbirds.

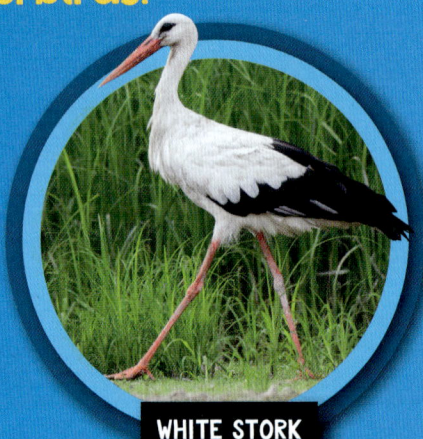

WHITE STORK

The rewilding of the Danube Delta offers a unique opportunity to restore a whole range of habitats including grassland, forest, freshwater marshes and coastal lagoons. The restoration of these ecosystems will also provide improved livelihoods for locals through wildlife tourism and sustainable fishing.

Restoration efforts include reflooding drained areas and reconnecting lakes to the Danube River. This will increase the wetland area and allow even more wildlife to thrive.

WATER BUFFALO

UKRAINE

SUCCESS STORIES...

The restoration of large islands in the **Danube Biosphere Reserve** has been one of the most successful wetland restoration projects in the region. Animals like the beaver and white-tailed eagle are already returning.

Pelican populations were hit hard by construction work and human activity in the delta throughout the twentieth century, but the **Pelican Way of Life** initiative, which began in 2019, has been building artificial nesting platforms to encourage vulnerable Dalmatian pelicans back into the area.

BEAVER

DID YOU KNOW?

Rewilding Europe are also supporting conservationists and partners affected by the war in Ukraine by shipping in vital resources.

DALMATIAN PELICAN

NORTH AMERICA

Find out about the successful **reintroduction** of **wolves** in **Yellowstone National Park** on page 64.

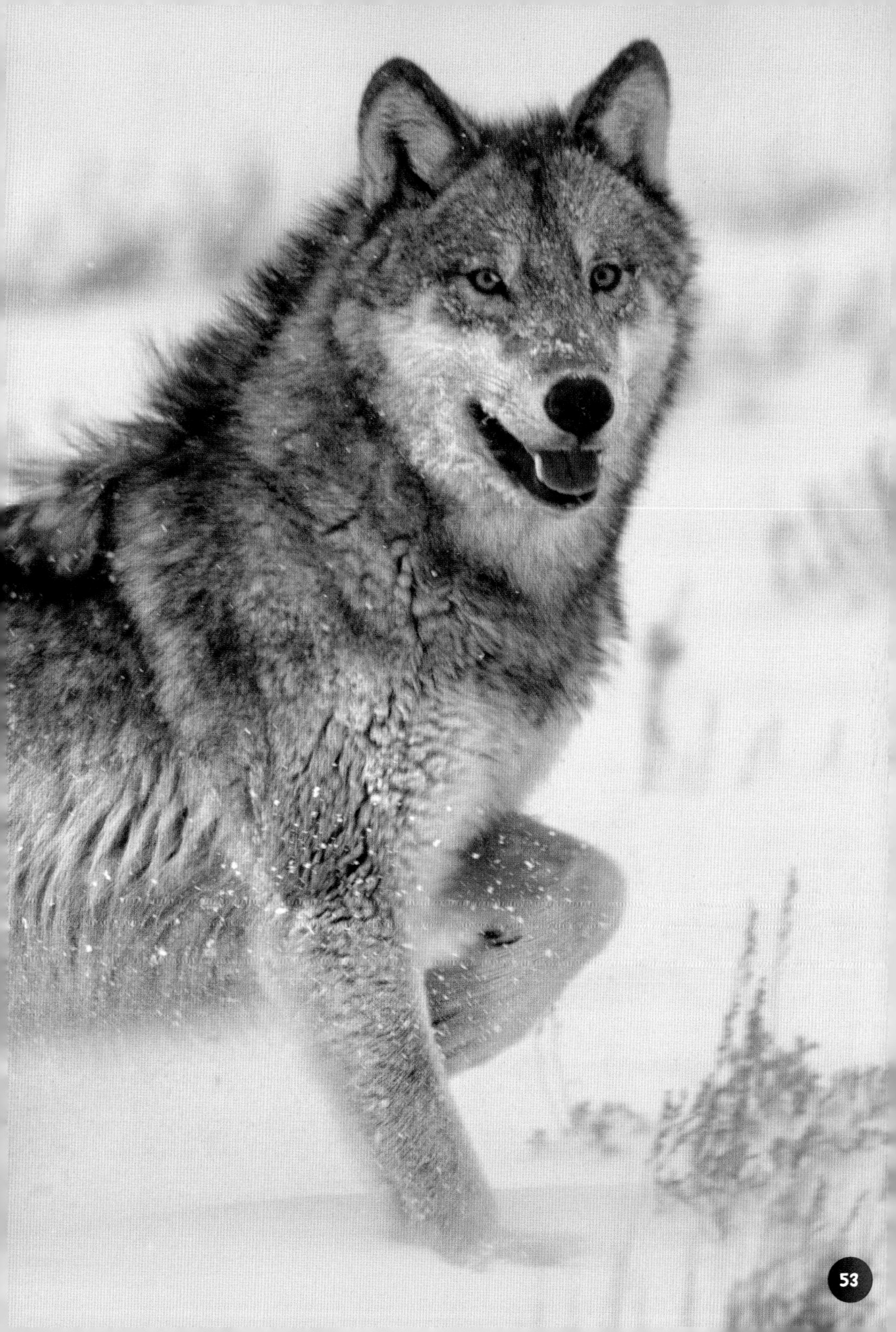

BOREAL SONGBIRD INITIATIVE

The Boreal Songbird Initiative's mission is to **protect boreal forest** across North America and the billions of **migratory birds** that rely on it.

DID YOU KNOW?

Boreal forests are named after the Greek god of the north wind, Boreas.

The boreal forest stretches across from Alaska, USA to Newfoundland, Canada and is vital for migratory birds as a place to breed and find food. Nearly half of the 700 bird species that can be seen in the USA and Canada rely on the boreal forest for survival.

During spring up to 3 billion birds migrate north to find suitable breeding grounds in the forest. Up to 5 billion then migrate south after breeding, and around 1 billion stay there over winter, making this landscape the largest wintering ground for birds such as the yellow-rumped warbler and rusty blackbird.

Although the majority of Canada's boreal forest remains undisturbed by human activity, much of the southern portion has been lost to commercial development. Industries including mining, timber, oil and gas are moving further into the forest, and if historic logging rates continue it is thought that over 60,000 square kilometres of forest will be lost in the next 10 years.

The boreal forest offers the best opportunity to implement large-scale habitat conservation as the forest remains mostly intact and over 6 million square kilometres.

RUSTY BLACKBIRD

CANADA AND UNITED STATES

«« YELLOW-RUMPED WARBLER

SUCCESS STORIES...

In 2020, Canada pledged to **protect** at least 17% of land across the country as part of the country's commitment to the Convention on Biological Diversity.

SAVING the AXOLOTL

DID YOU KNOW?
If injured, axolotls can regrow their limbs, organs and even part of their eyes!

The National Autonomous University of Mexico (UNAM) is **leading the way** in methods to help **save** the **environmentally** and **culturally** important **axolotl**.

The axolotl is a Critically Endangered aquatic salamander that can only be found in the wild in Lake Xochimilco in Mexico. Axolotls have faced major threats for decades. From 1998 to 2020, the axolotl population went from an average of 6,000 individuals per square kilometre to just 35.

The challenges these amphibians face have included the draining of part of the lake they live in (to help reduce flooding), which reduced the size of their habitat, pollution, and damage to habitat by boats. Rich nutrients from agricultural runoff have caused an excess of plant life on the water, starving the animals in the lake of oxygen. Also, fish such as tilapia were introduced to Lake Xochimilco. These fish prey on the axolotls' eggs and young, drastically reducing their numbers.

To help this iconic species recover, conservation efforts are focusing on restoring their habitat. This is being done by encouraging farmers to stop using harmful pesticides that could enter the lake, and instead to farm with traditional chinampas. These are floating island vegetable gardens made from aquatic vegetation and mud, which make ideal sanctuaries for axolotls.

Barriers are also being created to protect the axolotls from predatory, invasive fish, and awareness is being raised through schools and community outreach about ways to reduce disturbance by people in the axolotls' habitat.

AXOLOTL

MEXICO

SUCCESS STORIES...

The biologist **Luis Zambrano**, who is leading the way in axolotl conservation, is hopeful for the future of these animals as interest in saving them steadily increases, which he hopes will lead to further protection being granted by the government.

CREATING the MOGOLLON WILDLIFE CORRIDOR

The **Mogollon Rim** is a huge area of **mountains, rivers** and **forests** that stretches from the Gila Wilderness in New Mexico to the Grand Canyon in Arizona.

The Rewilding Institute and its partners have a vision for this extensive part of North America. Their aim is to protect and restore wild areas, creating a Mogollon wildlife corridor to protect biodiversity and tackle the effects of climate change.

At the moment, parts of the Mogollon 'wildway' are mapped out in full and protected by conservationists, but the full project would see around 4,500 square kilometres of four diverse habitats connected. These would range from the Rocky Mountains in the north to sub-tropical regions in the south and desert climates in the east and west.

Conservation methods include working with the US Forest Service to secure legal protection and save more wild forests from commercial logging.

Allowing nature to claim land to extend and connect habitats would benefit species such as the Mexican spotted owl, native fish like the Gila chub, and the reintroduced Mexican wolf. It would even provide suitable space to enable the return of the iconic jaguar.

MEXICAN SPOTTED OWL

UNITED STATES

SUCCESS STORIES...

Having been lost from the area for around 30 years, in 1998 the first captive-bred **Mexican wolves** were released into the Mexican Wolf Experimental Population Area in Arizona and New Mexico by the US Fish and Wildlife Service.

MEXICAN WOLVES

MOGOLLON RIM

RETURN of the BLACK-FOOTED FERRET

The **black-footed ferret** is one of the most endangered **mammals** in North America, but organisations such as the US Fish and Wildlife Service and WWF are working hard to **save** this species from **extinction**.

BLACK-TAILED PRARIE DOG

Twice during the twentieth century the black-footed ferret was thought to be extinct. The first time was due to the persecution of this predator's main prey, the black-tailed prairie dog. The prairie dogs were killed in such high numbers that they occupied just 2% of their historic range. Then, in the early 1980s, both the prairie dogs and the ferrets were devastated by a disease, sylvatic plague.

In 1981, a small wild population of the black-footed ferret was rediscovered in Wyoming. The impact of the disease meant this group contained only 18 individuals. Scientists brought the ferrets into captivity, and began what is now a successful captive breeding and reintroduction programme.

The reason this species of ferret is so dependent on the prairie dog is that they live exclusively in the burrows dug out by the rodents. The prairie dogs also make up over 90% of the ferret's diet.

As well as captive breeding and reintroduction programmes, conservationists are working to rewild and protect their habitat and reduce the spread of disease.

SUCCESS STORIES...

UNITED STATES

Due to successful captive breeding and releases, there are now over **700 black-footed** ferrets.

Organisations such as Southern Plains Land Trust are focusing on rewilding suitable habitat to help **new populations** of prairie dogs and black-footed ferrets as well as other wildlife.

DID YOU KNOW?

A dog called Shep was responsible for rediscovering the black-footed ferrets in Wyoming in 1981.

BLACK-FOOTED FERRET

SANTA MONICA MOUNTAINS

Re:wild and partners **planted** over **100,000** native **trees** and plants to bring back rich biodiversity in the Santa Monica Mountains.

The Santa Monica Mountains have hot, dry summers and cool, wet winters. They are home to animal and plant species that aren't found anywhere else on the planet and are part of a biodiversity hotspot known as the California Floristic Province.

Two massive wildfires burned huge areas of landscape in 2013 and 2018. The wildfire in 2018, known as the Woolsey Fire, spread through the region for more than a week. Around half of the Santa Monica Mountains were burned.

Since 2021, over 3,000 volunteers have helped plant native trees in the hope of restoring areas destroyed by the fires.

SANTA MONICA MOUNTAINS

WOOLSEY FIRE

UNITED STATES

MOUNTAIN LION

Volunteers prepared the damaged area for planting by clearing the land and drilling holes into the ground for seeds. New trees were protected from the elements and grazing animals, and healthy growth was encouraged by manual watering and weeding of unwanted species. There are now more than 1,000 plant species in the area, including unique native plants called dudleyas. Animals are also thriving, including the return of mountain lions and coyotes. There are almost 400 bird species that now call this region home.

SUCCESS STORIES...

One of the world's **largest wildlife crossings** is currently being constructed in the Santa Monica Mountains. This will help animals like mountain lions to expand their range and to avoid collisions with cars when moving to other suitable areas of habitat.

DID YOU KNOW?

Some species of plants in the Santa Monica Mountains are Critically Endangered, such as Verity's dudleya and the chocolate lily.

CHOCOLATE LILY

The WOLVES of YELLOWSTONE NATIONAL PARK

One of the most successful wildlife **reintroductions** and **rewilding** programmes in the US occurred in **1995** when a pack of **wolves** was released in **Yellowstone National Park**.

Grey wolves had been hunted to extinction in the area over a hundred years ago. Because the wolves are natural predators, animals such as Rocky Mountain elk and bison could reproduce without their numbers being controlled. This led to these herbivores overrunning and overgrazing the park, displacing smaller animals from their habitat and negatively impacting biodiversity.

Over two years between 1995 and 1997, 41 wolves were released, and all were tracked and studied so their impact on the surrounding environment could be measured.

ROCKY MOUNTAIN ELK

The hunting behaviour of the wolves reduced numbers of elk and changed the behaviour of these large browsing animals, so that they moved more quickly through feeding areas, rather than overbrowsing favoured spots. This allowed a range of trees and shrubs to grow, causing increases in bird and insect populations. Even beavers benefitted by being able to build more effective dams from the variety of trees now available.

BEAVER

BALD EAGLE

UNITED STATES

The wolves also killed coyotes. This meant smaller prey species could increase in number, which in turn, boosted numbers of birds of prey in the area.

DID YOU KNOW?

There are over 500 wolves living in Yellowstone National Park, all descended from the original pack.

GREY WOLF

SUCCESS STORIES...

The introduction of this **top predator** was so successful in Yellowstone that many places across Europe are using it as a framework in their own national parks.

65

SOUTH AMERICA

Find out about the **saving** of **giant tortoises** in the **Galapagos Islands**, Ecuador on page 74.

67

JAGUAR REINTRODUCTION PROJECT

DID YOU KNOW?

There are only around 173,000 jaguars left in the world, and most of them are found in the Amazon rainforest.

The Jaguar Reintroduction Project has a vision to **rewild** the Iberá wetlands, which were previously lost to ranch land. This would enable the return of a **keystone** species – **the jaguar** – which has been absent in the region for over **70 years**.

The Iberá National Park was established in 2018 after years of campaigning by conservation groups. Together with the Iberá Provincial Park, it forms part of a protected area of around 7,800 square kilometres, making it the largest nature park in Argentina.

Jaguars have been lost from 40% of their range across the Americas due to habitat loss, a reduction in prey species and conflict with local communities. As top predators, these big cats are fundamental in restoring balance to the ecosystem and sustaining healthy habitat in places like the Iberá wetlands.

In 2018, the Jaguar Reintroduction Project successfully bred jaguars at their breeding centre in Argentina. They could only be released into the wild when they were old enough and had been taught the skills required to survive on their own. In 2020, a group of young jaguars reared at the centre was released into the park and monitored.

The hope is that one day jaguar populations will once again extend across the Americas, from the southwestern tip of the USA, through Central America, to Patagonia in southern South America.

SUCCESS STORIES...

ARGENTINA

In 2022, **wildfires** devastated the Iberá parks despite efforts by organisations such as Rewilding Argentina to stop the destruction. Unbelievably, the eight jaguars released a few years before were all found alive, and conservationists were able to look after them until the fires were put out.

JAGUAR

BRINGING BACK the SPIX'S MACAW

A **global partnership** between the Brazilian Government and private organisations, led by the Association for the Conservation of Threatened Parrots (ACTP) is attempting to bring back the **Spix's macaw**.

This majestic blue bird, made famous in 2011 by the film Rio, was last seen in its native forest habitat in 2000. It was officially declared extinct in the wild in October 2019. Captive breeding has been carried out over many years, involving the few remaining individuals. The population is now at a level where birds can be reintroduced to the wild.

SPIX'S MACAW

BRAZIL

The first trial population of around 20 Spix's macaw was released in 2022, with further reintroductions planned over the next 20 years. At the same time, native vegetation will be restored, providing more suitable habitat for the parrots to safely expand into.

The semi-arid vegetation found in this part of Brazil is home to many unique species, as well as providing important habitat for the Spix's macaw. It is susceptible to climate change and is threatened by overgrazing. This type of habitat destruction contributed to the decline and eventual extinction of this species of parrot. The project aims to restore around 17,000 hectares of forest, and encourage local people to reduce grazing pressure by livestock and to manage the habitat sensitively.

Today, around 160 Spix's macaws exist in professional parrot breeding facilities. Most of the birds bred for release into the wild are cared for at the ACTP breeding centre.

DID YOU KNOW?

The Spix's macaws were released alongside another parrot species to help them learn how to survive in the wild again.

SUCCESS STORIES...

Thanks to decades of research and conservation efforts by scientists, conservationists, vets and indigenous people, the Spix's macaw is now flying **free in the wild** once again, and there is renewed hope for its future.

PATAGONIA NATIONAL PARK PROJECTS

The **Tompkins Conservation** team have worked throughout the **Patagonia region** of South America to conserve and rewild habitat, restore **biodiversity** and **reduce conflict** between **wildlife** and local **communities**.

The Chacabuco Valley in Chile's Patagonia National Park is a natural corridor through the Andes. In the past, this region has suffered from overgrazing because of livestock being moved through the area and large sections of the region being used as ranch land.

CHACABUCO VALLEY

In a large grassland restoration project, conservationists worked to buy land from ranchers, remove livestock, take down hundreds of kilometres of fencing and restore plant life in the area. The team also led the way in the reintroduction and protection of native animals such as mountain lions, Andean condors, Darwin's rheas and huemul deer.

DARWIN'S RHEA

CHILE

HUEMUL DEER

Camera traps and new wildlife corridors are being used to monitor and help the Endangered huemul deer, which is unique to the Andes. An estimated 1,500 live in broken populations, so connecting the areas where they live will help this species better survive threats such as illegal hunting and wildfires.

SUCCESS STORIES...

In 2022, two **Andean condors** were released in the park with satellite transmitters attached to track their movements. This information has helped Tompkins Conservation target their efforts to protect the species more effectively.

DID YOU KNOW?

60,000 square kilometres of Patagonia National Park is now completely protected thanks to organisations such as Tompkins Conservation.

ANDEAN CONDOR

The GIANT TORTOISES of the GALÁPAGOS

The saving of the giant tortoises in the Galápagos Islands has been one of the most successful efforts by conservation groups to bring back an animal from the brink of extinction using rewilding methods.

Two hundred years ago there were over 200,000 giant tortoises roaming the Galápagos Islands, but by the first half of the nineteenth century they were almost wiped out. Passing whalers and sailors hunted the tortoises as an easy food source. More recently, their main threat has been from habitat destruction and invasive species such as rats, which ate the tortoises' eggs, and goats which outcompeted them for food.

As 'ecosystem engineers' these herbivores are crucial to the environment. Each tortoise eats more than 200 kilograms of vegetation every year, and they spread seeds through their droppings. This increases the biodiversity of plant life and maintains healthy ecosystems throughout the Galápagos.

Ten of the islands each have their own subspecies of giant tortoise. In the 1960s, only 15 individuals of the Española giant tortoise remained. This small group was taken into captivity where they could breed safely. This process of captive breeding and release back into the wild was so successful that there are now over 2,000 of them.

Despite this progress, populations are still just 10% of their previous levels and only occupy 35% of available habitat. Galápagos Conservancy are working with the Galápagos National Park Directorate, with a vision to restore the remaining giant tortoise species population to their historical range. Based on results so far, this vision seems to be on the path to success.

SUCCESS STORIES...

ECUADOR

Captive rearing has been used in Galápagos since 1965 to help restore nine of the eleven surviving species of giant tortoise. By the end of 2017, more than 7,000 juvenile tortoises had been returned to their islands of origin — including Española, Isabela, Pinzón, San Cristóbal, Santa Cruz and Santiago.

DID YOU KNOW?

More species of tortoise and turtle can be found in and around the Galápagos Islands than anywhere else in the world.

GIANT TORTOISE

THE AMAZON RIVER DOLPHIN

River dolphin numbers are falling due to habitat destruction and pollution, but WWF is trying to **reverse** the population decline by looking at how best to **conserve** them and the rivers they live in.

The Amazon river dolphin lives in freshwater rivers throughout the Amazon and Orinoco river basins in Brazil, Colombia, Venezuela and neighbouring countries. Their numbers have been threatened by habitat loss and contamination of the waters they live in. Mercury pollution from people mining for gold in rivers is a major threat to the Bolivian subspecies.

The dolphins are also at risk from people as they are seen as competitors to fishing communities. The catfish that they prey on is in high demand in Brazil, and the dolphins are often killed or injured when driven away from precious fish stocks. They are also hunted despite it being illegal to harm them.

WWF is working to protect and preserve habitats where the river dolphin is found and is carrying out important surveys to monitor population sizes. It is thought there is a population size in the low tens of thousands, but it is challenging to count the dolphins in the murky streams where they live.

Due to the many threats facing these dolphins and the difficulty in monitoring them, organisations are finding it almost impossible to count them. However, with the help of locals, many are now being captured and tagged before being returned to the river. This vital data will support efforts to protect them in the future.

AMAZON RIVER DOLPHIN

SOUTH AMERICA

DID YOU KNOW?

The Amazon river dolphin is also known as the pink river dolphin or 'boto'.

SUCCESS STORIES...

A review of more than **300,000 kilometres** of rivers in the Amazon basin has been conducted to gather information on migratory fish and turtles. This has helped map important routes used by animals like the river dolphin, and conservationists can now work to keep river channels free from dams and other obstructions, so that the animals can move freely between different habitats and areas.

SAVING the TAPIR

The Tapir Specialist Group work to **study** and **protect tapirs** and the habitat they occupy, in **Central** and **South America** and Southeast Asia.

Three species of tapir occupy forest, grassland and swampy areas in Central and South America. Once widely abundant, all three species have now been classified as either Vulnerable or Endangered because of habitat destruction. Their forest habitat has been cleared to make way for rearing livestock and mining, and they have also fallen victim to hunting.

The tapir is an important animal. As they move through the forest, tapirs disturb the ground and spread seeds in their droppings. This helps to regenerate the forest and helps in the reproduction of slow-growing trees, which are vital for capturing carbon from the atmosphere. This makes the tapir a crucial species in the fight against climate change, as their actions result in the growth of more trees.

When farmers move into tapirs' territory, the animals eat their crops. This brings them into conflict, and in retaliation many farmers will hunt the tapir. This is now negatively impacting tapir populations. The Tapir Specialist Group are researching the crop-raiding behaviour of the tapir and developing strategies to discourage it. This will reduce conflict and save these animals from further threats of hunting.

Tapirs have large territories, with each lowland tapir occupying a range equivalent to 500 football pitches. When conservationists secure protection for these animals, they therefore also conserve huge chunks of habitat, to the benefit of other plants and wildlife.

SUCCESS STORIES...

CENTRAL AND SOUTH AMERICA

The Lowland Tapir Conservation Initiative is having real success saving lowland tapirs from road collisions by using **speed cameras** and educational signs.

TAPIR

DID YOU KNOW?

Tapirs are South America's largest land mammal.

AFRICA

Find out about the **return** of **cheetahs** and other animals to **Phinda Game Reserve**, South Africa, on page 94.

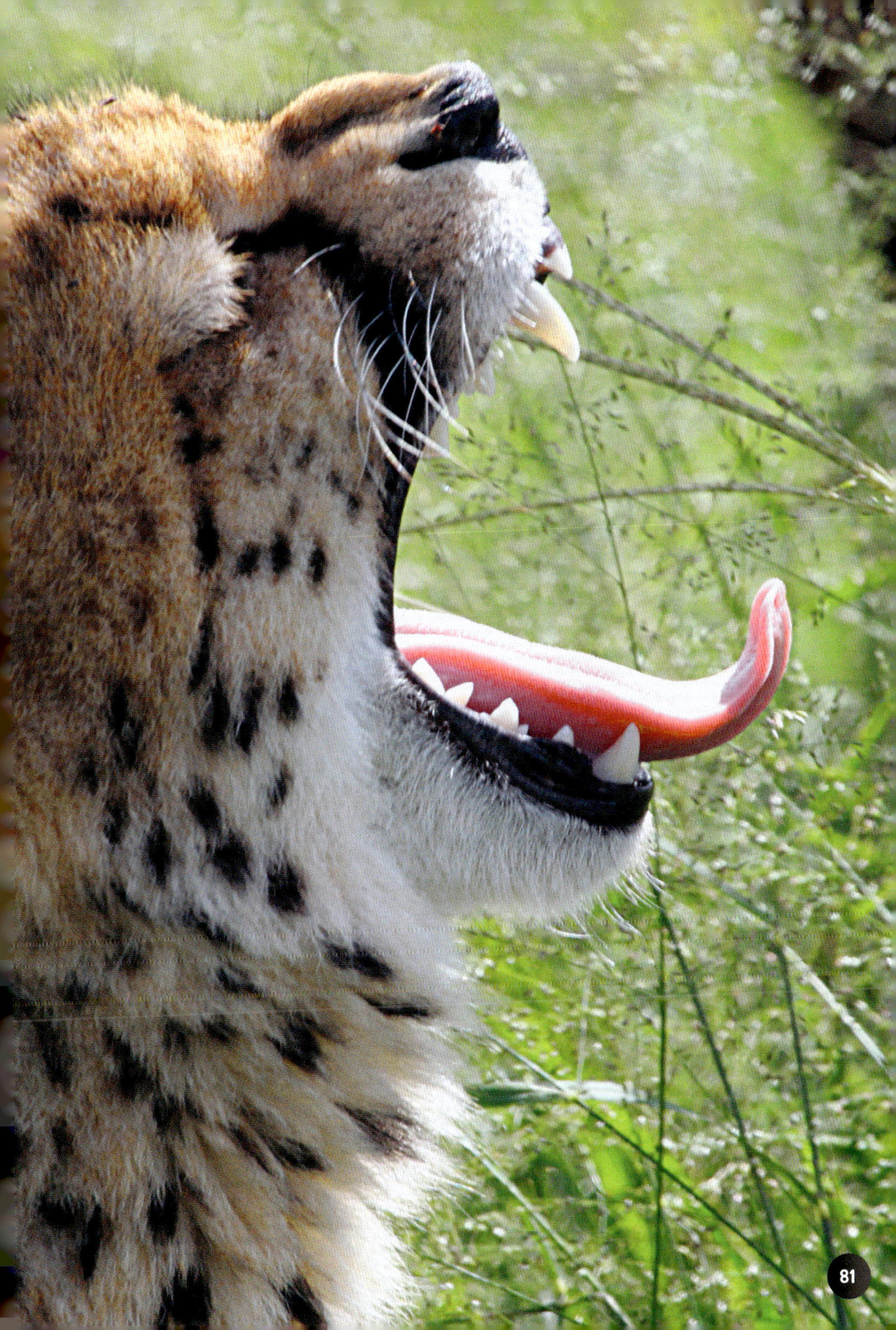

PROTECTING the OKAVANGO DELTA

The **Okavango Delta** is a unique **ecosystem** supporting hundreds of thousands of local people. It is a vital water source for some of the world's most **threatened** wildlife and a landscape so **huge** it is visible from space.

The Okavango Delta is an oasis in the Kalahari Desert. It is one of very few river deltas that don't flow into the ocean, instead being made up of marshland and floodplains that evaporate water directly into the air. It is also unique in that the yearly flooding from the Okavango River occurs during the dry season, acting as a lifeline to many animals during the hottest part of the year.

OKAVANGO DELTA

ELEPHANT HERD

BOTSWANA

This flood season provides a vital water source in a desert environment for species such as lions, giraffes and elephants (the largest herd on the planet), so any risk of the water becoming contaminated would have devastating impacts on the ecosystem.

The delta relies completely on rivers flowing through other countries, such as Namibia, before emptying into northern Botswana. Besides climate change, human activity further upstream is the main threat to the preservation of the delta. Pollution from fertilisers, deforestation and removing too much water for human use are all significant risks.

Together, community trusts and conservation groups have sought to protect as much of the land as possible and raise awareness of the importance of keeping the river system and delta healthy and intact.

LIONS

SUCCESS STORIES...

The Okavango Delta was declared a **World Heritage Site** in 2014, the 1000th World Heritage Site listing across the globe, which ensures international conservation protection.

DID YOU KNOW?

The delta has more than 1,000 islands — some just a few metres wide, but others longer than 10 kilometres!

PROTECTING ZAKOUMA NATIONAL PARK

Zakouma National Park in **Chad** was once a stronghold for over **4,000 elephants**, but **90%** of the park's elephants were lost to **poaching**. Conservation groups have worked hard over the last **10 years** to reverse this.

By 2010, many of the elephant herds in Zakouma had been lost to poachers targeting them for ivory. The Government of Chad negotiated a long-term agreement with conservation organisations to manage the national park, rewild habitat there and protect the last 500 elephants that roamed the landscape.

Elephants are targeted by poachers for their ivory tusks, which are sold illegally to places where there is a high demand. The tusks are often made into sculptures and are seen as a symbol of wealth.

Through community engagement and the introduction of stricter laws against wildlife crime, biodiversity began to increase in the park. By 2016 poaching had almost been eliminated, and Zakouma has become a place of safety for Endangered animals.

CHAD

SUCCESS STORIES...

Zakouma's success in protecting elephants and other wildlife has led to the creation of jobs in the tourism industry and to manage the reserves. The national park is now the **largest employer** for local people, directly helping communities living in the area.

ELEPHANTS

DID YOU KNOW?

There are now around 650 elephants in Zakouma National Park.

SAVING THE GORILLAS
of the DRC

Conservationists have been monitoring the movements and behaviour of wild **eastern lowland gorilla** in the Democratic Republic of the Congo's Tayna Nature Reserve. They hope to better **protect** these **endangered** animals in their **natural** habitat.

Habitat destruction and civil unrest in the country means wild eastern lowland gorilla populations have decreased by 80%. This means around 6,800 individuals are left, making this primate one of the most endangered. Tayna Nature Reserve is one of the last places left where larger groups of gorillas can survive.

The Gorilla Rehabilitation and Conservation Education (GRACE) Centre is the world's only rescue centre for eastern lowland gorillas. The rehabilitation team there nurse orphaned, sick or injured gorillas back to health and teach them the necessary survival skills before reintroducing them into the wild once.

Conservation teams track the gorillas on foot due to the density of the forest and always stay at least a day's travel behind the group to reduce disturbance to these highly sensitive animals. Scientists collect data to learn more about their behaviour, diet and movements. Genetic information from poo samples is also extracted in order to identify individual gorillas and monitor their health.

SUCCESS STORIES...

In 2020, the first ever **survey of gorillas** was carried out across the reserve and it confirmed healthy populations of this animal existed in Tayna.

DEMOCRATIC REPUBLIC OF THE CONGO

EASTERN LOWLAND GORILLA

DID YOU KNOW?
The eastern lowland gorilla is also known as Grauer's gorilla.

AFRICAN WILD DOG REINTRODUCTION IN MALAWI

DID YOU KNOW?
There are fewer than 7,000 African wild dogs left in the wild.

African wild dogs were **reintroduced** to the Liwonde National Park and Majete Wildlife Reserve in Malawi by African Parks and their partners. This is the **first time** these animals have been in the country for **60 years**.

Wild dogs have decreased across Africa due to disease, hunting and poisoning; they are the second most endangered carnivore on the African continent. Their reintroduction is part of a larger project to rewild Malawi.

VULTURE

Reintroductions of other large predators, lions and cheetahs, in Liwonde National Park resulted in the return of four species of vulture returning naturally. The vultures consume carcasses and help stop the spread of diseases among local people and their livestock.

LION

MALAWI

WILD DOG

Fourteen wild dogs in two packs were brought to Malawi — eight to Liwonde National Park and six to Majete Widlife Reserve.

Both packs of wild dogs were fitted with radio and satellite collars to track their movements. Sadly, in 2022 tragedy struck in Liwonde: the pack was found dead, having all been poisoned. To help prevent more dogs being lost to poisoning, as happened in Liwonde, African Parks have focused on providing poison awareness training to local communities. In turn, local people benefit from tourists visiting to see predators such as wild dogs.

WILD DOGS HUNTING

SUCCESS STORIES...

The **six wild dogs** taken to Majete continue to thrive. They have successfully raised several litters of pups since their release and are positively shaping the habitat around them.

REWILDING RWANDA

Akagera National Park was almost destroyed by the Rwandan **Civil War** in the **1990s**. Thanks to conservation efforts, much of the park has been **restored** to its former glory and iconic **African animals** are now returning.

After the conflict ended, people living in the area had little choice but to turn to Akagera's habitats for timber, to graze their livestock and hunt wildlife for bushmeat.

In more recent years, conservation groups have taken action to save what was left of the park and rewild it for the future.

One of the most successful conservation efforts was the reintroduction of the black rhino in 2017. Eighteen eastern black rhinos made the 4,000-kilometre journey from South Africa, followed by five more from Europe in 2019. In 2022, they were joined by 30 southern white rhinos.

African Parks led the restoration of the national park and reintroduction of the rhinos in the hope of not only increasing biodiversity throughout the landscape but of attracting tourists too. Tourism is key for the long-term conservation and protection for Akagera National Park with money made from tourism going directly back to helping native wildlife and local communities.

AKAGERA NATIONAL PARK

RWANDA

BLACK RHINO

SUCCESS STORIES...

Conservationists took part in years of research and training in how to track and monitor the introduced rhinos in order to keep them safe from poachers while living in the park.

DID YOU KNOW?
There are estimated to be only 6,000 black rhinos left in the wild.

PANGOLIN ZULULAND CONSERVATION TRUST

Pangolins are the world's most **trafficked** animal and are in danger of being **poached** to extinction. Zululand Conservation Trust is an organisation working to **rescue, rehabilitate** and **protect** these incredible mammals.

Pangolins' only defence in the wild is to roll into a ball and lay still, unfortunately making them an easy target for poachers. They are then taken from the wild and their scales are used in traditional medicines across Asia.

SUCCESS STORIES...

Since 2019, over **15 pangolins** have been successfully rehabilitated in Zululand after being rescued from poachers, with five wild pangolin pups having been born there.

SOUTH AFRICA

Manyoni Private Game Reserve is working with vets and conservation groups to rescue trafficked pangolins, nurse them back to health and put them back into the wild in protected areas.

Rescued pangolins are checked every day to monitor their weight and overall health before undergoing what's called a 'soft release'. This is where resources like food and water are initially provided for them until they establish their own territory and can forage for food themselves. Temminck's pangolin hasn't roamed Zululand for 70 years, so bringing them back into suitable habitat there is great news for the region.

DID YOU KNOW?

Pangolins have been around for over 80 million years.

PANGOLIN

PHINDA GAME RESERVE

DID YOU KNOW?
Phinda means 'the return' in Zulu.

The reserve is home to Africa's **'Big Five'** (lions, leopards, elephants, buffalo and rhinoceros), along with over **400 bird species**, cheetahs and **antelope**.

Wildlife always roamed across this region, but for many decades until 1991, the land was damaged by overgrazing by cattle. Now, through successful rewilding, this protected area contains a mixture of habitats, including woodland, grassland, mountains, rivers and wetlands.

Local people have been consulted and involved in the transformation of Phinda to a rewilded landscape that attracts tourists. The benefits for local communities, which include education and medical facilities as well as jobs and incomes, have led to community-owned land being added to the reserve.

Over the 30 years since the creation of the reserve, &Beyond and Munywana Conservation have expanded Phinda to more than double its original size.

In one of the largest translocation projects of its kind, **21 white rhinoceroses** were moved to Phinda in a single day!

SUCCESS STORIES...

SOUTH AFRICA

Phinda is the first private reserve to reintroduce **elephants.**

Cheetahs were introduced to the reserve in 1993 which helped boost population numbers across the country.

More than **70 leopards** were radio collared between 2002 and 2012, with the data collected leading to a reduction in trophy hunting and an increase in the local population.

ELEPHANT

WHITE RHINOCEROSES

ASIA

Find out about **conservation** efforts to protect **Critically Endangered orangutans** in Borneo on page 100.

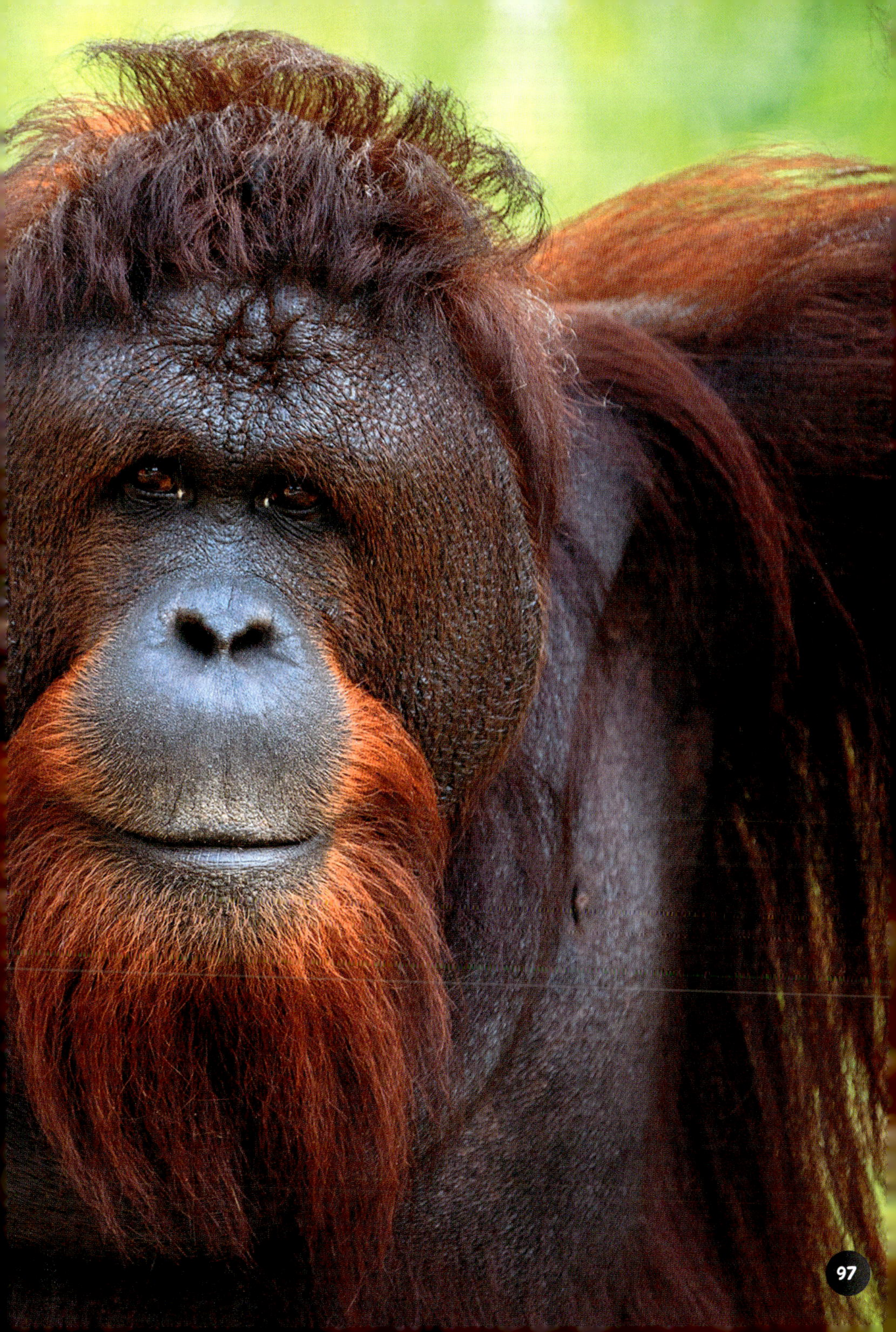

PYGMY HOGS of MANAS NATIONAL PARK

Over the last 15 years, captive-bred **pygmy hogs** have been **released** at three sites in Assam, India, by the Pygmy Hog Conservation Programme (PHCP). The programme hopes to **restore** their numbers in the area where the last of their wild population **survives**.

In 1996, six hogs (two males and four females) were taken from the wild to start a breeding programme in the hope that this species could be saved from extinction.

The breeding programme was successful and reintroduction of captive bred hogs began in 2008. Three areas where pygmy hogs live naturally were selected and their alluvial grassland habitat was restored. Over the next 10 years over 100 hogs were released in stages at the three sites. Most recently, 36 pygmy hogs have been reintroduced at Manas National Park.

Pygmy hogs declined because their habitat has been turned into farmland. They are one of the first species to disappear when their habitat changes; if they are present in an area, scientists know the habitat is healthy, so it will be benefitting other species too.

Pygmy hogs are also extremely shy and spend most of their time hidden in the tall, dense grass, which makes them difficult to find. Despite this, monitoring has shown that the number of pygmy hogs has been steadily increasing each year. This is great news for conservationists and the future of this animal.

SUCCESS STORIES...

INDIA

The **reintroduction** in one of the three areas, Orang National Park, has been particularly successful as the hog population there is now more than double its original size.

The number of reintroduced pygmy hogs is now higher than the total number before conservationist stepped in.

PYGMY HOG

DID YOU KNOW?

The pygmy hog is the smallest and rarest pig species in the world.

PRIMATES in PERIL

DID YOU KNOW?
Young orangutans will spend about 7 years with their mum learning everything they need to know about surviving on their own.

One of our closest primate relatives, the **orangutan**, faces significant **threats** to its forest home. Conservation groups are working with local government bodies to better **protect** orangutans through **reintroductions** and reversing the damaging effects of human activity in their habitat.

Orangutans occupy a tiny 20% of their original habitat, mainly due to the clearing of forests for human use. All three species of orangutan (Bornean, Sumatran and Tapanuli) are Critically Endangered. While there were once well over 230,000 of these primates, there are now around 104,000 Bornean, 7,500 Sumatran and a dangerously low 700 Tapanuli left in the wild.

SUMATRAN ORANGUTAN

In Borneo, re:wild are supporting Borneo Nature Foundation in preventing the intentional peat-swamp fires that occur every year to make room for plantations (specialised farms). These human-caused fires destroy large areas of crucial habitat and release huge amounts of carbon stored in the peatlands into the atmosphere.

BORNEAN ORANGUTAN

BORNEO

In Sumatra, conservation groups are working together to preserve and rewild native habitat, not just for the orangutan, but also for the Critically Endangered Sumatran rhino and Endangered Asian elephant populations. As well as fighting to expand forested areas, they help to rehabilitate injured orangutans and release them back into the forests.

The Tapanuli orangutan has sadly joined the list of 'World's Most Endangered Primates' which includes the western chimpanzee and slow lorises, among others. They are currently at risk from a planned hydroelectric dam that, if built, would have terrible consequences for this species. Conservation bodies are therefore campaigning against the project.

SUMATRAN RHINO

SUCCESS STORIES...

In 2017, scientists successfully demonstrated that the **Tapanuli orangutan** was its own species (it used to be considered Sumatran). This information has led to targeted conservation and legal protection for the Tapanuli.

TAPANULI ORANGUTAN

SAVING the SAIGA

In 2006, **conservationists** came together to **save** the grasslands of the **Altyn Dala** in Kazakhstan and help stop the rapid decline of the Critically Endangered **saiga antelope**.

The Altyn Dala Conservative Initiative (ADCI) is undertaking a truly ambitious project, rewilding thousands of square kilometres of landscape. They are doing this through a combination of habitat protection, species research, wildlife crime prevention and raising awareness in local communities.

Poaching, disease and habitat loss caused the saiga antelope population to fall. Towards the end of the 1990s, hunting was completely banned, which provided welcome relief to the saiga population. In 2015, however, a virus spread through the remaining herds, killing 200,000 animals.

One of the challenges is that the antelope migrate huge distances each year, so protecting them along their migratory route can be extremely difficult. Not all of the 750,000 square kilometres occupied by saiga antelope can be protected, but important areas can be identified and conservation efforts focused there.

Conservationists are using satellite collars, drones and camera traps to monitor the herds on their travels. Scientific studies are also being carried out to build up a more detailed knowledge of the landscape, so that it can be rewilded to benefit not just the saiga, but other animal and plant species too.

KAZAKHSTAN

SAIGA

DID YOU KNOW?
Kazakhstan is home to 97% of the world's population of saiga antelope.

SUCCESS STORIES...

ADCI has helped the saiga by removing physical barriers, rewilding its steppe habitat and creating wildlife corridors so that migration routes are safer.

As well as the saiga, ADCI are working to bring back the kulan — a wild, horse-like animal that is also Critically Endangered back to the Altyn Dala steppe.

TIGERS in LAOS

WWF-Laos is embarking on a conservation strategy to recover Indochinese tiger populations throughout the country.

Laos is one of 13 countries where tigers roam, although it is thought there are now none occupying its forests as the last documented sighting of this big cat was via a camera trap in 2013. Up until the early 1980s there was a viable population in Laos, but habitat destruction and overhunting of the tiger's prey caused numbers to fall rapidly.

In 2022, WWF launched a 5-year conservation programme aimed at the protection and recovery of several key species, including the tiger.

Laos has the potential to support a population, which will ultimately boost global recovery efforts. Despite there being no evidence of tigers living in the country at the moment, there is enough intact habitat for them to return.

The next step is to reduce threats that reintroduced tigers would face, one of the most immediate being snares. These are used by poachers and wildlife traffickers, and it is thought that there are over 12 million snares in protected areas across some of the tiger's range in Asia. Snares not only pose a risk to tigers themselves but are a major threat to their prey species too.

By working in partnership and raising awareness among local communities to support the Indochinese tiger, there's hope that in the near future it will return to Laos.

DID YOU KNOW?

Without a population in Laos, the Indochinese tiger now only survives in Thailand and Myanmar.

LAOS

INDOCHINESE TIGER

SUCCESS STORIES...

WWF-Laos has been focusing conservation efforts in the west of the country in the Nam Poui National Protected Area. It has promising numbers of prey, wildlife corridors established to breeding populations of tigers in Thailand, and additional protections that will hopefully allow tigers to return.

PRZEWALSKI'S HORSE

DID YOU KNOW?
The Przewalski's horse is a distinct species of horse found in Asia that has never been domesticated.

The **Przewalski's horse**, a species that was near **extinction**, is now recovering in the wild across parts of **Asia** thanks to persistent conservation efforts spanning several **decades**.

Wild populations of Przewalski's horse declined due to European explorers hunting them for food and taking them from the wild to keep in private collections. They also suffered habitat loss and were pushed out of areas by people grazing livestock. These threats became so significant that the Przewalski's horse became extinct in the wild in the late 1960s.

By 1947, just 13 animals out of the 32 that were held in captivity could breed, and so the wild Przewalski's horses that exist today are all descended from that last known group.

By the early 1980s, due to breeding success, conservationists began to look for suitable habitat in order to reintroduce this species into the wild. Since then, reintroduction projects have been established in Mongolia, China and Ukraine.

The Gobi B Nature Reserve is one of the places where captive-bred Przewalski's horses are released. It is a landscape that includes desert environment with rocky plains and plenty of water sources to support herds through summer.

MONGOLIA

SUCCESS STORIES...

In 2016, the **Great Gobi 6 Initiative** was founded for government authorities, scientists and wildlife conservationists to discuss the best ways to maintain the Gobi B Nature Reserve in Mongolia and protect species including the Przewalski's horse, wild Bactrian camel and Gobi bear.

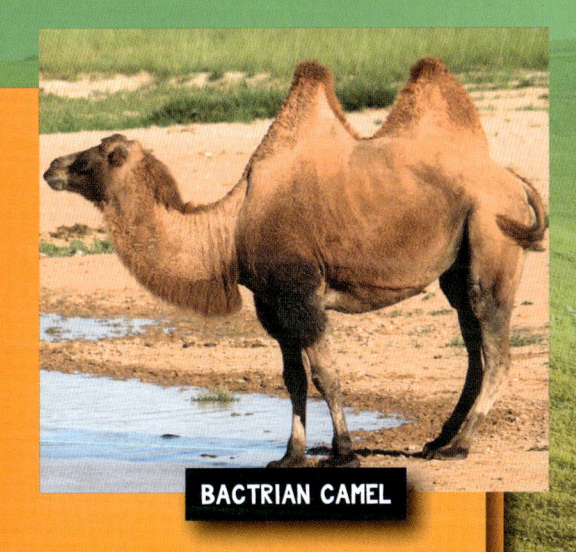

Since 1997, **Przewalski's horses** have been successfully breeding in the wild there is now a wild population of around 400.

BACTRIAN CAMEL

PRZEWALSKI'S HORSES

OCEANIA

Find out about how projects are **helping protect** Australia's **Great Barrier Reef** from **climate change** on page 116.

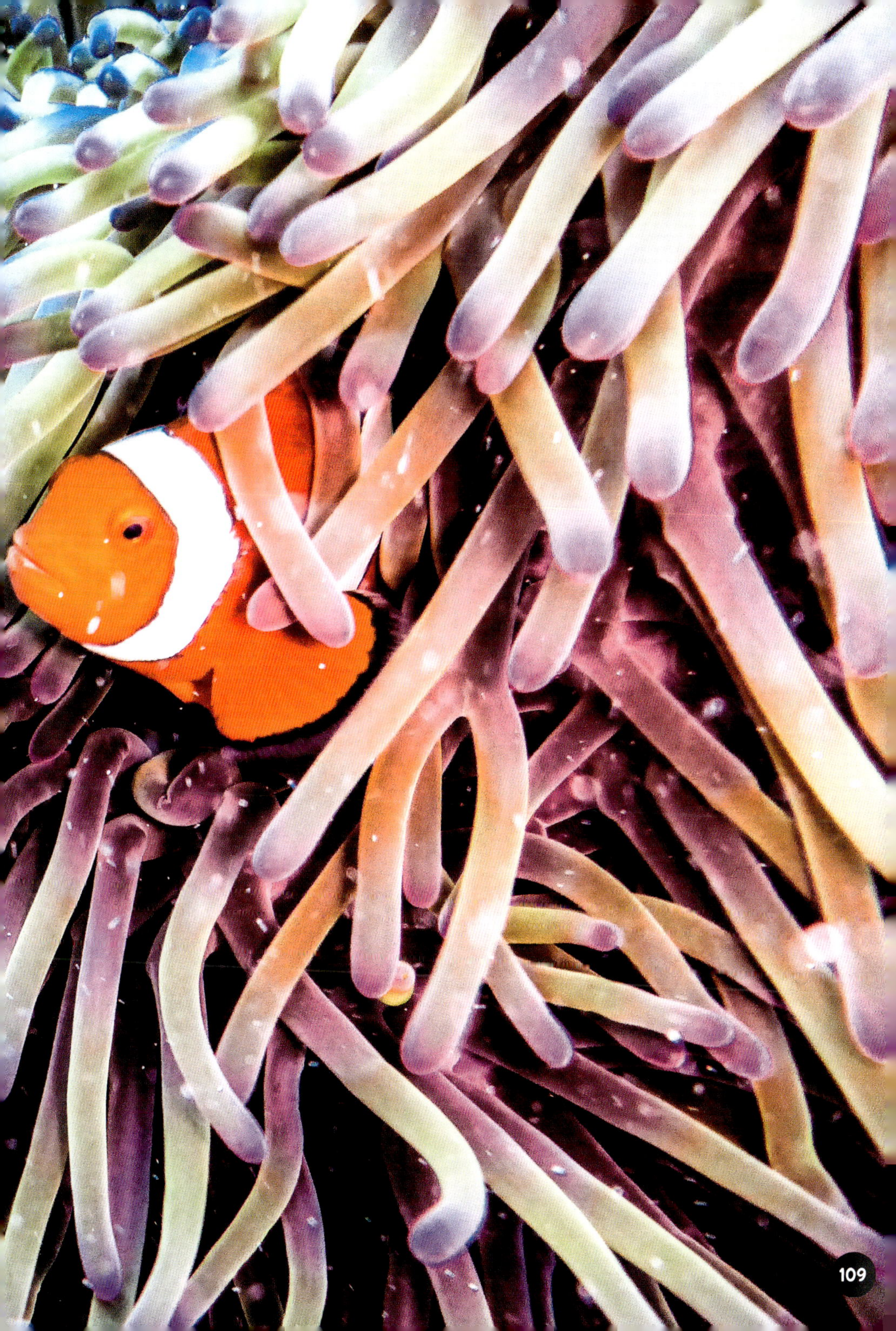

Bringing BACK the BRUSH-TAILED BETTONG

WWF-Australia is bringing back one of the country's rarest marsupials, the brush-tailed bettong, to an area they have been absent from for more than a century.

The brush-tailed bettong disappeared from South Australia's Yorke Peninsula at the start of the twentieth century due to habitat loss and the release of introduced predators, such as foxes and feral cats by Europeans. Conservationists are now working to bring the bettong back to a part of its historic range.

These rabbit-like animals, which look like mini kangaroos, once inhabited 60% of mainland Australia but are now Critically Endangered.

Their reintroduction to South Australia began in 2021 when a small group of 120 bettongs were captured from other areas in Australia and released into Dhilba Guuranda-Innes National Park.

The success of reintroducing the bettong in this area has been closely monitored by conservationists. The released bettongs have been fitted with radio-tracking collars to help in assessing their progress.

Nearly half of the bettongs captured during monitoring in 2022 were determined to have been born on the peninsula, showing they are successfully reproducing. The original released group are clearly comfortable in their new environment, finding food and raising young to adulthood.

Returning bettongs to this landscape will create a healthier habitat. Their behaviour of foraging for fungi in the ground turns over the soil, improving its quality and encouraging new seed growth. It is estimated a bettong can dig 2–6 tonnes of earth each year!

BRUSH-TAILED BETTONG

AUSTRALIA

DID YOU KNOW?
The brush-tailed bettong is also known as the 'yalgiri' or 'woylie'.

SUCCESS STORIES...

Marna Banggara is a project that hopes to **restore native wildlife** lost in parts of Australia. It hopes to reintroduce more species to the Yorke Peninsula through rewilding programmes, including the southern brown bandicoot, western quoll and red-tailed phascogale.

The RETURN of the TASMANIAN DEVIL

Through a **successful** rewilding programme, the **Tasmanian devil** has returned to mainland **Australia** for the first time in **3,000 years**.

In 2020, 26 Tasmanian devils were introduced to a secure area on Barrington Tops in New South Wales, Australia.

This key species has an important role in the ecosystem. Small but fierce, these predators push invasive foxes and cats out of areas, relieving pressure on the small native mammals they prey upon. The small mammals turn over soil as they look for food, burying leaves and spreading seed as they go, which regenerates the forest and reduces the intensity of wildfires. Tasmanian devils also reduce disease by scavenging and picking off sick prey. This disperses seeds and buries leaf litter, which helps reduce the intensity of wildfires and regenerate forests. As top predators, Tasmanian devils also keep the habitat free from disease by picking off sick prey.

Tasmanian devils vanished from mainland Australia at around the same time as dingoes spread throughout the continent, although the precise reason for the devils' decline is unclear. They still populated Tasmania (an island state of Australia), which dingoes never made it over to, but have faced threats from hunting. In addition, a fatal disease called Devil Facial Tumour Disease (DFTD) devastated Tasmanian devils' numbers there. The disease has wiped out 90% of wild Tasmanian devils, and fewer than 20,000 remain.

Conservationists are working to expand protected areas of forest on the mainland, in preparation for the return of more Tasmanian devils and other endangered animals in a massive rewilding project that hopes to restore some of Australia's most iconic wildlife.

DID YOU KNOW?

Tasmanian devils get the 'devil' part of their name from the blood-curdling screams they emit when trying to scare off other animals.

SUCCESS STORIES...

AUSTRALIA

Scientists are carefully monitoring the recently reintroduced Tasmanian devils. If the group adapt well to their new environment, more Tasmanian devils will be introduced using the same strategy, creating populations in different areas around Australia.

Some Tasmanian devils have developed resistance to DFTD, so conservationists are focusing on these populations for reintroduction efforts.

TASMANIAN DEVIL

The KAKI of NEW ZELAND

With only **150 left** in the wild, the kaki is **Critically Endangered**, but thanks to a **breeding** programme, **numbers are climbing.**

The kaki, or black stilt, has become the world's rarest wading bird (a bird that forages for food in shallow water). The species quickly declined due to habitat destruction, human disturbance and the introduction of non-native predators. Feral cats and ferrets predated eggs, and young and adult birds.

Efforts by the Department of Conservation (DOC) to protect the species began in 1981 when the population of kaki dropped to just 23 wild individuals. Over the next few decades scientists worked hard to save the kaki from extinction.

Towards the end of 2019, the DOC expanded the breeding programme by increasing the number of chicks that could be hand-reared. Now that the programme can hatch and raise more chicks, over 100 birds can be released each year. In addition, by controlling the number of invasive predators, conservationists can boost the survival rate for released chicks from 30% to over 50%.

As well as releasing individuals into the wild, organisations are working together to fund a large-scale project to restore and rewild the landscape where kaki currently live. They aim to gradually expand the protected area to enable the kaki population to flourish further.

With the support of landowners, scientists and the general public, it is hoped that kaki will thrive in their natural environment once again.

NEW ZEALAND

<<< KAKI

DID YOU KNOW?
Within hours, newly hatched chicks can forage for food and swim.

SUCCESS STORIES...

Nearly all of today's **Kakis** were initially reared in captivity. Without this conservation intervention they would have become extinct.

Another organisation called Predator Free NZ is working to eradicate all ferrets, rats and other small **invasive predators** from New Zealand by 2050.

REEF RESTORATION and ADOPTION

The **Great Barrier Reef** is one of the world's **seven natural wonders** and the **largest coral reef** system on the planet.

DID YOU KNOW?
Coral looks like a plant, but its structure is in fact made up of thousands of tiny invertebrate animals (animals without a backbone) called polyps.

Coral reefs play a vital role in the health of Australia's oceans. At least a quarter of animals in the ocean need coral reefs during their life, whether for food, shelter or to reproduce.

The reef is under threat from overfishing, pollution and coral bleaching. Over the last seven years there have been four major bleaching incidences. In March 2022 a bleaching incident saw 91% of the reef impacted.

Coral bleaching is caused by warmer water temperatures, and climate change is increasing the temperature of the world's oceans. This casuses the coral to become stressed and release the algae they live in partnership with, and which give them their colour, into the water. Bleaching leaves these once beautiful corals drained of colour, rock hard and dying.

BLEACHED CORAL

SUCCESS STORIES...

AUSTRALIA

A **healthy reef** can recover, if it is given time and in the right conditions. Reef Restoration and Adaptation Programme (RRAP) is helping the Great Barrier Reef 'resist, adapt and recover' from the impacts of climate change. They are using techniques suchs as shading the coral (using sea spray to create a cloud above the reef to deflect light from the Sun), bonding together damaged parts of the reef which help it to regrow, and providing human-made structures to increase suitable area on the ocean floor for coral to settle.

THE GREAT BARRIER REEF

ANTARCTICA

Find out about the **sanctuary** for **whales** in **Antarctica's Southern Ocean** on page 120.

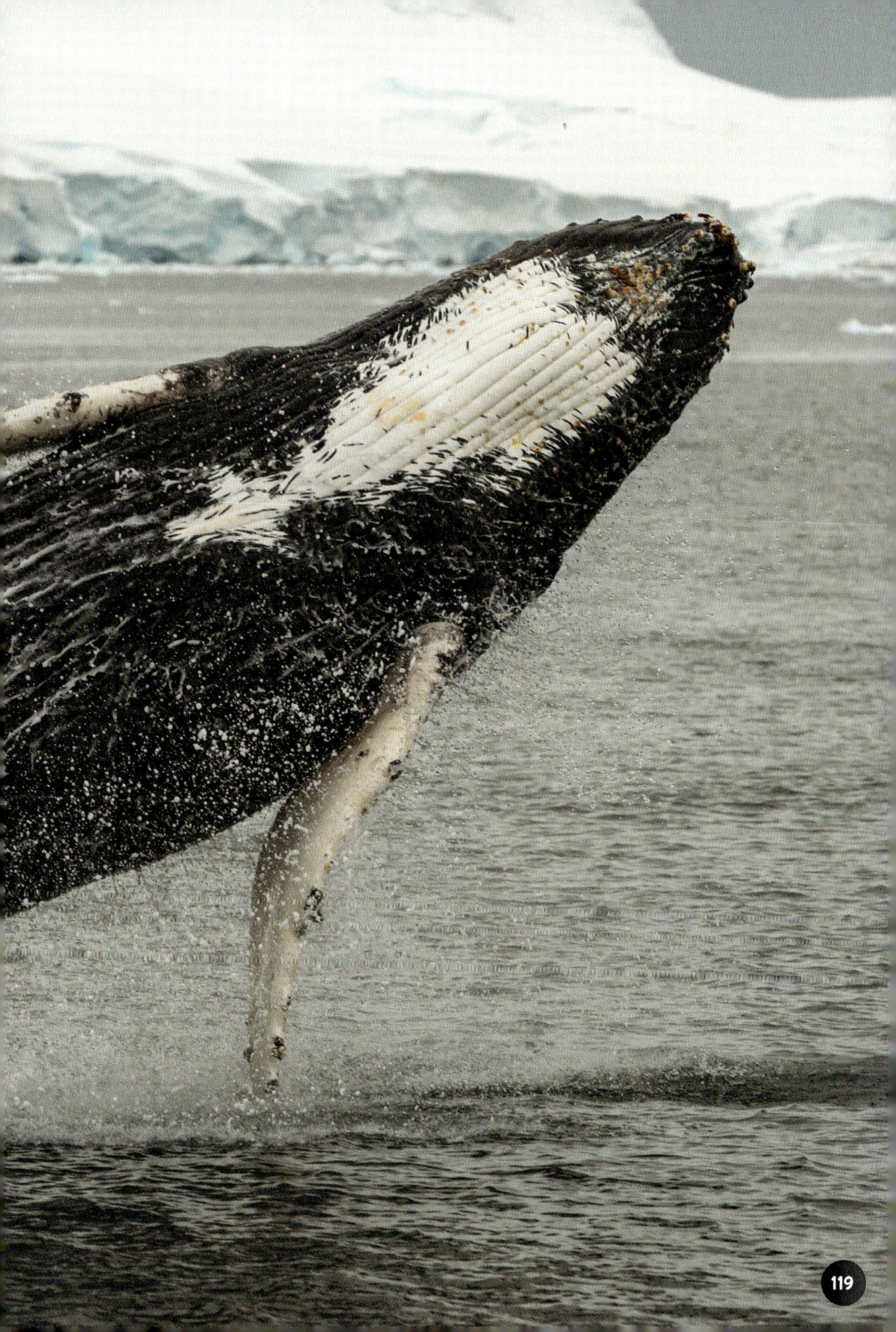

SAVE the WHALES

The Southern Ocean **Whale Sanctuary** surrounds the entire continent of **Antarctica**, and all types of commercial **whaling** have been **banned** there by the International Whaling Commission (IWC).

Two sanctuaries are currently under the protection of the IWC — one in the Indian Ocean, which was established in 1979, and one in the Southern Ocean, adopted in 1994.

Many species of whale are endangered and these large mammals play a vital role in regulating ocean habitat, so protecting them is important.

Whales also help fight climate change in a weird and wonderful way — through their poo! When whales poo they spray large quantities of faeces into the ocean. Their poo is full of nutrients from the bottom of the ocean, where they feed, which they then release nearer the surface. These nutrients help tiny marine organisms called phytoplankton grow in number — much like a fertiliser does for plants. Phytoplankton produce oxygen and capture large amounts of carbon from the atmosphere.

DID YOU KNOW?

The marine sanctuaries offer protection to species such as the blue whale, humpback whale and southern right whale.

ANTARCTICA

Despite a ban on all whaling in these protected areas, Japan continued to hunt minke whales within the sanctuary boundaries, for scientific reasons, up until 2019. This controversial practice led to disputes between scientists, conservationists and politicians.

MINKE WHALE

The biggest threat to whales, however, isn't whaling, but pollution. Plastic pollution and discarded fishing gear kill hundreds of thousands of dolphins and whales each year, so preserving pristine marine habitat is important to help populations recover.

WATER POLLUTION

SUCCESS STORIES...

Conservationists are tackling these threats to whales by using both short-term and long-term strategies. Efforts to clean up the ocean are being carried out alongside initiatives to establish more marine reserves in our oceans.

BLUE WHALE

GLOSSARY

arid
Arid land is so dry that very few plants can grow on it.

awareness
Someone who is aware understands that their behaviours and actions can have an impact on the environment around them.

biodiversity
Biodiversity includes the wide variety of all living things, especially when they are living in their natural environment.

browse/browsing
Browsing animals feed on the leaves and shoots of shrubs and trees.

captive breeding
Captive breeding is the breeding of wild animals in places such as zoos, often of animals which have become rare in the wild.

colonisation
When plants and animals colonise a place, they spread into it and make it their home.

competition
Animals compete with one another for resources such as food or mates.

conservation (of wildlife)
Conservation is saving, protecting and maintaining the natural environment.

contamination
Contamination occurs when organisms, or the environment in which they live, are exposed to harmful or toxic substances which can make them sick.

Critically Endangered
A Critically Endangered species is one that faces an extremely high risk of extinction in the wild.

ALL THREE SPECIES OF ORANGUTAN ARE CRITCALLY ENDANGERED.

deforestation
If an area is deforested, all the trees there are cut down or destroyed.

delta
A delta is an area of land shaped like a triangle that forms where a river ends — often when it meets a sea, lake or reservoir — or is blocked by a geographical feature.

demonstration site
A demonstration site is a place where humans show how it is possible to improve an area for wildlife, including reintroducing species that had previously gone extinct.

eco-friendly
Eco-friendly means living in a way that is earth-friendly or not harmful to the environment.

ecosystem
An ecosystem is a community of wild species, including plants and animals, living in a natural environment and interacting in a natural way.

ecosystem engineer
An organism that has an important role in changing and maintaining their surrounding habitat and other wildlife within it.

Endangered
An Endangered species is one that faces a very high risk of extinction in the wild.

DALMATIAN PELICANS CAN BE FOUND IN THE DANUBE DELTA.

endemic species
A species that is only found in one part of the world, and nowhere else.

environment
The environment is the natural world including land, sea, water, air, plants and animals.

establish (to become established)
A non-native species becomes established when they are introduced to a new habitat and settle there for a long time.

extinction
The extinction of a species means that all of its members have died and it is lost from the Earth forever.

fledge
To fledge means to feed and care for a young bird until it is able to fly.

COWS ON THE RIVER WAAL FLOODPLAIN IN THE NETHERLANDS.

floodplain
A floodplain is the area around a river which is covered in water when there is a flood.

forage
When animals forage, they search for food.

genetic diversity
Genetic diversity refers to all the different genes contained in a living species.

genetic information
The genetic information of an organism refers to all of its biological information that is passed on from one generation to the next.

graze/grazing
When animals graze, they eat grass or other low-growing plants.

habitat
The habitat of an animal or plant is the particular kind of natural environment in which it normally lives or grows.

herbivore
A herbivore is an animal that only eats plants.

historical range
The historical range of a species refers to the geographical areas in which they used to live in the past.

hybrid
A hybrid is an animal or plant that has bred from two different species of animal or plant.

indigenous
Indigenous species belong to a place and live there naturally, rather than being brought there from another country.

introduction
A species that is or has previously been brought to a place that it does not live in naturally.

keystone species
A keystone species is one which has a very large impact on its ecosystem. If a keystone species is removed, the ecosystem could collapse.

GALÁPAGOS TORTOISES ARE HERBIVORES.

landscape
The landscape is everything you can see when you look across an area of land, including hills, rivers, buildings, trees and plants.

REINDEER MIGRATION IN SWEDEN.

migration
Migration is the movement of a species usually in search of food or to a good place to breed, which often happens every year according to the seasons.

migratory
A migratory creature is one that migrates every year.

monitor
Humans can monitor changes in the environment or the health of a population.

native
Species that are native to a particular region live or grow there naturally and were not brought there.

native breed
A native breed is a type of domestic livestock that is especially suited to a particular geographical region.

natural range
The natural range is the geographical area over which a species has naturally lived in recent times.

natural regrowth
Natural regrowth is the process by which trees, shrubs and other plants self-seed and spread.

nature tourism
Nature tourism is travel to natural areas, often to see special wildlife or habitats.

old-growth (forest)
An old-growth forest is a forest that has developed over a long period of time and has never been damaged by people.

outcompete
Plants and animals outcompete each other if they succeed in getting more resources, such as food or mates.

overgrazing
Overgrazing happens when too many animals, often farm livestock, are allowed to eat vegetation in a particular area, which damages the environment.

population
A population is the number of a particular type of plant, animal or other species that is present in a certain area.

THE GREY WOLVES IN YELLOWSTONE NATIONAL PARK ARE PREDATORS.

predator
A predator is an animal that kills and eats other animals.

radio or satellite/tracking
Radio and satellite transmitters fitted to animals send signals that allow researchers to find the animals and track their movements to learn about their behaviour.

WILD DOGS IN MALAWI ARE MONITORED USING RADIO TRACKING.

reclaim
Land that has been used by humans can be reclaimed for nature.

recovery (of species or habitat)
Recovery is when damaged places become healthy again or lost species of plants and animals return to it.

rehabilitation
Rehabilitation helps sick, injured or orphaned wild animals so that they may survive when released back into their natural habitat.

reintroduction
Reintroduction happens when organisms are brought back into an area after the native population has become extinct.

reproduction
Reproduction is the bioglogical process by which an organism produces offspring.

restoration
Restoration is the return of an ecosystem or habitat to its natural state.

rewet
To make something wet again, especially wetlands such as bogs or marshes that have been drained or dried out due to people's activities.

rewilding
Rewilding is the practice of allowing nature to take care of itself and letting areas of land return to their wild state.

scavenger
A scavenger is any animal that feeds on dead plants and animals.

spawning ground
A spawning ground is a place where fish lay their eggs for fertilisation.

species
A species is a class of organisms, such as plants or animals whose members have the same main characteristics and are able to breed with each other.

subspecies
Subspecies are subgroups within a species, often found in different geographical locations, which are genetically a bit different from each other.

survey
A survey of a species or place is the gathering of information or data, which researchers use to understand the health of the population of that species or the habitat.

sustainability
Sustainability refers to the ability to responsibly use natural resources, so that they never run out and can continue to be used in the future.

translocation
Translocation is the movement of living organisms from one place to another.

viable (population)
A population of species is viable if it has enough genetic diversity to produce healthy offspring over a long period of time, without help from humans.

wetland
A wetland has water at or close to the surface and a community of special plants and animals living in it.

wildlife corridor
Wildlife corridors are passages of habitat or cover that allow species to move safely over larger distances and areas of habitat.

SURVEYS OF GORILLAS HAVE TAKEN PLACE AT TAYNA NATURE RESERVE IN DEMOCRATIC REPUBLIC OF THE CONGO.

Acknowledgements

Publisher: Michelle l'Anson
Head of Creative Services: Craig Balfour
Text: Heather Ryce
Typesetter: QBS
Editorial: Frances Cooper, Julianna Dunn, Lauren Reid
Cover Design: Sarah Duxbury

Image Credits

Cover
Front (t) Fercast/Shutterstock; (m) Mark Medcalf/Shutterstock; (b) blickwinkel / Alamy Stock Photo; Spine FRDMR/Shutterstock; Back cover (t) Mikadun/Shutterstock; (m) Oleksii G/Shutterstock; (b) Donovan van Staden/Shutterstock

Internal
P3 Mark Medcalf/Shutterstock; P4 (t) Gail Johnson/Shutterstock; (ml) Sandra Kenyon/Shutterstock; (mr) Agnieszka Bacal/Shutterstock; (b) FOTOGRIN/Shutterstock; P5 (t) Matt Ragen/Shutterstock; (mr) jeep2499/Shutterstock; (ml) Benedikt Juerges/Shutterstock; (b) Philipp Salveter/Shutterstock; P6 Gail Johnson/Shutterstock; P9 (t) Digital Wildlife Scotland/Shutterstock; (b) Stephen John David Wain/Shutterstock; P10 SeraphP/Shutterstock; P11 ArCaLu/Shutterstock; P12 (m) PhotosWales/Shutterstock; (b) matushaban/Shutterstock; P13 (t) Michal Pesata/Shutterstock; (m) Stephan Morris/Shutterstock; (b) Stephan Morris/Shutterstock; P14 Eduardo Estellez/Shutterstock; P15 (t) Matt Sumner/Shutterstock; (m) PJ photography/Shutterstock; (b) Mark Anthony Ray/Shutterstock; P16 (t) Erik Mandre/Shutterstock; (m) mountaintreks/Shutterstock; P17 (t) Michele Aldeghi/Shutterstock; (b) Ian W Douglas/Shutterstock; P18 Libor Fousek/Shutterstock; P20 Mark Medcalf/Shutterstock; P23 Giedriius/Shutterstock; P24 Vladimir Wrangel/Shutterstock; P26 Sandra Kenyon/Shutterstock; P28 (m) Sergej Razvodovskij/Shutterstock; (b) Martin Prochazkacz/Shutterstock; P29 (t) Martin Prochazkacz/Shutterstock; (m) Smeerjewegproducties/Shutterstock; (b) Martin Prochazkacz/Shutterstock; P30 Victor Suarez Naranjo/Shutterstock; P32 crystaldream/Shutterstock; P33 (t) Tai Dundua/Shutterstock; (m) Sylvia Bruning/Shutterstock; (b) Nicole Kwiatkowski/Shutterstock; P35 Daniel Doorakkers/Shutterstock; P37 Alauddin Abbasi/Shutterstock; P38 (m) Bo Scheeringa Photography/Shutterstock; (b) Bo Scheeringa Photography/Shutterstock; P39 (t) Erni/Shutterstock; (b) Carlos Pereira M/Shutterstock; P40 Gennaro Leonardi Photos/Shutterstock; P41 Gennaro Leonardi Photos/Shutterstock; P42 E.Duif/Shutterstock; P43 Anton Havelaar/Shutterstock; P45 (t) Tomas Calle Boyero/Shutterstock; (b) Jesus Cobaleda/Shutterstock; P47 LuisMiguelEstevez/Shutterstock; P48 evgenii mitroshin/Shutterstock; P50 (t) Leon Kiss/Shutterstock; (b) S.Borisovich/Shutterstock; P51 (t) Willant.Zoltan/Shutterstock; (b) Ondrej Prosicky/Shutterstock; P52 Agnieszka Bacal/Shutterstock; P54 Krumpelman Photography/Shutterstock; P55 Daniel Zuckerkandel/Shutterstock; P57 Narek87/Shutterstock; P58 Rob Palmer Photography/Shutterstock; P59 (t) GoodFocused/Shutterstock; (b) Hugh Hull/Shutterstock; P60 Jolanda Aalbers/Shutterstock; P61 Kerry Hargrove/Shutterstock; P62 (m) Lando Aviles/Shutterstock; (b) Morphius Film/Shutterstock; P63 (t) sirtravelalot/Shutterstock; (b) C. Rene Ammundsen/Shutterstock; P64 (m) Ariena/Shutterstock; (b) Kris Wiktor/Shutterstock; P65 (t) Richard Seeley/Shutterstock; (b) Agnieszka Bacal/Shutterstock; P66 FOTOGRIN/Shutterstock; P69 Jo Reason/Shutterstock; P70 Danny Ye/Shutterstock; P72 (m) Gambarini Gianandrea/Shutterstock; (b) Victor Suarez Naranjo/Shutterstock; P73 (t) Olena Viktorova/Shutterstock; (b) BearFotos/Shutterstock; P75 FOTOGRIN/Shutterstock; P77 COULANGES/Shutterstock; P79 Uwe Bergwitz/Shutterstock; P80 Michelle Cavanagh/Shutterstock; P82 (m) evenfh/Shutterstock; (b) Gaston Piccinetti/Shutterstock; P83 (t) Thomas Retterath/Shutterstock; P85 Thomas Clode/Shutterstock; P87 PhotocechCZ/Shutterstock; P88 (t) Henk Bogaard/Shutterstock; (b) Matt Starling Photography/Shutterstock; P89 (t) Cheryl Jayaratne/Shutterstock; (m) Cheryl Jayaratne/Shutterstock; P90 Thomas Bartelds/Shutterstock; P91 Emma Geary/Shutterstock; P92 nwdph/Shutterstock; P93 Simon Eeman/Shutterstock; P95 (t) Matt Ragen/Shutterstock; (b) Johan1966/Shutterstock; P96 jeep2499/Shutterstock; P99 Yvdalmia/Shutterstock; P100 (m) Sertan Yaman/Shutterstock; (b) Milan Zygmunt/Shutterstock; P101 (t) Supriadi Pramela/Shutterstock; (b) Wirestock Creators/Shutterstock; P103 Yakov Oskanov/Shutterstock; P105 PUMPZA/Shutterstock; P106 (t) Chursina Viktoriia/Shutterstock; (b) AleksandrSch/Shutterstock; P107 (t) Alexandr33/Shutterstock; (b) Zazaa Mongolia/Shutterstock; P108 Benedikt Juerges/Shutterstock; P111 Martin Pelanek/Shutterstock; P112 Susan Flashman/Shutterstock; P113 Oleksii G/Shutterstock; P115 Glenda Rees/Shutterstock; P116 William Edge/Shutterstock; P117 ChameleonsEye/Shutterstock; P118 Philipp Salveter/Shutterstock; P121 (t) Annie Leblanc/Shutterstock; (m) Mr.anaked/Shutterstock; (b) Andrew Sutton/Shutterstock; P122 Sergey Uryadnikov/Shutterstock; P123 gergosz/Shutterstock; P124 (t) E.Duif/Shutterstock; (b) Maridav/Shutterstock; P125 longtaildog/Shutterstock; P126 (t) Wildpix productions/Shutterstock; (b) Piotr Poznan/Shutterstock; P127 Asaf Weizman/Shutterstock.